The Best of Stories

By
Shaykh Mufti Saiful Islām

JKN Publications

© Copyright by JKN Publications

First Published in February 2020

ISBN 978-1-909114-48-7

British Library Cataloguing in Publication Data
A catalogue record for this book is available from the British Library.

Publisher's Note:

Every care and attention has been put into the production of this book. If however, you find any errors they are our own, for which we seek Allāh's ﷻ forgiveness and the reader's pardon.

Published by:

JKN Publications
118 Manningham Lane
Bradford
West Yorkshire
BD8 7JF
United Kingdom

t: +44 (0) 1274 308 456 | w: www.jkn.org.uk | e: info@jkn.org.uk

Book Title: The Best of Stories

Author: Shaykh Mufti Saiful Islām

Printing by Mega Printing in Turkey

"In the Name of Allāh, the Most Beneficent,
the Most Merciful"

Contents

Introduction

Verily all praise is for Allāh ﷻ. He is my Lord and your Lord. By Him we were created and to Him we shall return. Our worship can never praise Allāh ﷻ the way He truly deserves, yet through His divine mercy, we hope for it to be accepted from us.

Allāh ﷻ blessed us with faith. This is undeniably the greatest blessing we hold. The Noble Qur'ān that we recite, study and implement, along with the carefully preserved sayings and actions of the Final Prophet Muhammad ﷺ act as our compass in this life, to reach our destination - Jannah (Paradise). Therefore, it is absolutely vital to follow these accordingly and as best as we possibly can. May Allāh ﷻ make this book a means of doing so. Āmīn!

Alhamdulillāh, by the grace of Allāh ﷻ, I have been truly fortunate to compile a book on the Tafsīr (commentary) of a particular Sūrah of the Qur'ān Karīm. Sūrah Yūsuf is more than just a story of one of our beloved Prophets ﷺ, there is much wisdom and lessons to be learnt and understood. All the knowledge comes from our honourable Shaykh, inspiration and Ustādh, Shaykh Mufti Saiful Islām Sāhib. May Allāh ﷻ shower Mufti Sāhib with mercy and accept the day in, day out effort he carries out in the work of Dīn. Āmīn!

Dhākirah Ali
Student of Jāmiah Khātamun Nabīyeen
January 2020/Jumādal- Ūlā 1441

Background

Sūrah Yūsuf is in the 12th chapter of the Holy Qur'ān. It contains a total of 111 verses, forming 12 Rukus. As it was revealed to the Holy Prophet ﷺ in Makkah Mukarramah, it is known as a Makkan Sūrah.

This Sūrah was revealed whilst the Holy Prophet ﷺ was going through much hardship, during the tenth year of prophethood. His beloved wife, Sayyidah Khadījah ﵂ had passed away and not so long after, his beloved uncle, Abū Ṭālib also passed away. The Holy Prophet ﷺ named this year, the 'Year of Grief'. For this reason, Allāh ﷻ revealed Sūrah Yūsuf to console and cheer up the Holy Prophet ﷺ.

For all those people who are going through any kind of hardship, whether it be grief, misery, depression or illness etc., it is advisable to read Sūrah Yūsuf in abundance. Inshā-Allāh it will bring joy, relief and perseverance during times of distress.

$$ الٓرٰ ۚ تِلْكَ اٰيَاتُ الْكِتَابِ الْمُبِيْنِ $$

[1] Alif Lām Rā. These are the verses of the Clear Book.

The Sūrah starts of with Alif Lām Rā, these are known as isolated letters or Hurūf Muqaṭṭa'āt. The meaning of these letters are only known to Allāh ﷻ, which is why the scholars of Tafsīr (Mufassirūn) state 'Allāh ﷻ knows best', whenever they encounter Hurūf Muqatta'āt.

Allāh ﷻ describes the verses in the Holy Qur'ān as 'Mubīn'. The verb pattern that 'Mubīn' originates from means, to make something clear and apparent. Therefore, in terms of these verses we are reciting, there is absolutely no confusion, ambiguity or misunderstanding. Everything is extremely clear because Allāh ﷻ has made it so.

One question that the polytheists of Makkah Mukarramah would ask the Ahle Kitāb (People of the Book) regarding Sayyidunā Yūsuf ﷺ was, how he had arrived in Egypt. They knew he was originally from Palestine but didn't understand how he ended up in Egypt. This Sūrah was partly revealed on account of this.

The Beauty of Arabic

$$ إِنَّا أَنْزَلْنَاهُ قُرْآنًا عَرَبِيًّا لَّعَلَّكُمْ تَعْقِلُونَ $$

[2] Indeed We have revealed it as an Arabic Qur'ān so that you will understand.

Allāh ﷻ revealed the Holy Qur'ān in the Arabic language because the first addressees were Arabs. The Holy Prophet ﷺ and the Sahābah Kirām ﷺ spoke Arabic, hence it made sense to address them in their language so that they understand.

Arabic is a very eloquent and articulate language, perhaps the most eloquent of all. There are so many intricacies that emerge from a single word, it is so encompassing. It is also a very easy language to learn, along with Urdu. Allāh ﷻ has made it complete, comprehensive and concise in every aspect.

The Prophet ﷺ is reported to have said:

أَحِبُّوا الْعَرَبَ لِثَلَاثٍ لِأَنِّي عَرَبِيٌّ وَالْقُرْآنُ عَرَبِيٌّ وَكَلَامُ أَهْلِ الْجَنَّةِ عَرَبِيٌّ

"Love the Arabic language for three reasons; because I am an Arab, the language of the Qur'ān is Arabic and the language of the people of Jannah is Arabic." (Shu'bul Imān, Mustadrak Imām Hākim)

Furthermore, Imām Ibn Kathīr ﷦ has famously said,

أُنْزِلَ أَشْرَفُ الْكُتُبِ عَلَى أَشْرَفِ الرُّسُلِ بِأَشْرَفِ اللُّغَاتِ بِسِفَارَةِ أَشْرَفِ الْمَلَائِكَةِ، وَكَانَ اِبْتِدَاءُ نُزُوْلِه فِيْ أَشْرَفِ بِقَاعِ الْأَرْضِ وَهُوَ فِيْ أَشْرَفِ شُهُوْرِ السَّنَةِ فَكَمُلَ مِنْ كُلِّ الْوُجُوْهِ

"The most noble Book (i.e. the Qur'ān) was revealed in the most noble language (i.e. Arabic) upon the most noble Messenger (i.e. the Prophet ﷺ) through the medium of the most noble Angel (i.e. Jibrīl عليه السلام) in the most sacred place of the world (i.e. Makkah Mukarramah) in the most noble of months (i.e. Ramadhān). Hence, it is complete in every aspect."

These are just a few reasons of why we should be interested in learning Arabic, in particular Classical Arabic. It will connect us to the Holy Qur'ān and Aḥādīth because we can reflect on the deep meanings, and truly understand what our Lord is commanding us to do.

The Best of Stories

نَحْنُ نَقُصُّ عَلَيْكَ أَحْسَنَ الْقَصَصِ بِمَا أَوْحَيْنَا إِلَيْكَ هَٰذَا الْقُرْآنَ وَإِنْ كُنْتَ مِنْ قَبْلِهِ لَمِنَ الْغَافِلِينَ

[3] We narrate to you the best of all stories because of what We have revealed towards you of this Qur'ān and indeed you were prior to this, from those who were not informed.

A unique aspect of this Sūrah which is different to others, is how it is the only story which continues until it finishes. Here, Allāh ﷻ has narrated the *whole* story of Sayyidunā Yūsuf عليه السلام, from the very beginning to the end. Stories from the lives of other Prophets عليهم السلام such as Sayyidunā Harūn عليه السلام, Sayyidunā Ismāīl عليه السلام and Sayyidunā Ibrāhīm عليه السلام etc. have been scattered in different parts of the Holy Qur'ān.

Allāh ﷻ is notifying us that He has given us this Qur'ān and through this Qur'ān, He is going to narrate this wonderful story to us. The word Allāh ﷻ uses to describe the story is 'ahsan' which means, very good, the best. 'Ahsan' is that story which contains good morals for everybody and therefore, we will be able to take beneficial lessons from the story of Sayyidunā Yūsuf ﷺ. Also, the best of stories can refer to the fact that there will be no lies or fabrications, because it is Allāh ﷻ Who has revealed it. Furthermore, in the story every individual's ending turns to be positive and fruitful, hence the best of stories.

These days, people make up stories just to make people laugh. Some can even go to the extent in believing there is no Allāh ﷻ. Any person who does not believe in life after death, they will surely be saying:

وَقَالُوْا لَوْ كُنَّا نَسْمَعُ أَوْ نَعْقِلُ مَا كُنَّا فِيْٓ أَصْحَابِ السَّعِيْرِ

"If only we had been listening or reasoning, we would not be among the companions of the Blaze." (67:10)

On the Day of Judgement, everybody who had not accepted Islām in the worldly life will be filled with regret. They may be perceived by the world as very intelligent by holding titles such as 'Professor' or 'Doctor', but if they have not come to the conclusion that there is a Divine Creator, in the eyes of Allāh ﷻ and the Holy Prophet ﷺ he is a fool.

Allāh ﷻ says in one verse:

يَعْلَمُوْنَ ظَاهِرًا مِّنَ الْحَيَاةِ الدُّنْيَا وَهُمْ عَنِ الْاٰخِرَةِ هُمْ غَافِلُوْنَ

11

They know what is apparent of the worldly life, but they are unaware of the Hereafter. (30:7)

Allāh ﷻ tells the Holy Prophet ﷺ that before this revelation, he was from those people who were not informed. In other words, before this revelation (Wahī), the Holy Prophet ﷺ did not know about the story of Sayyidunā Yūsuf السلام عليه, hence he was being informed through Wahī.

This is strong evidence proving that the Holy Prophet ﷺ was not عَالِمُ الْغَيْب because if he was, what would be the need to reveal this Sūrah? He would have known it already.

Why did the Holy Prophet ﷺ go through so much hardship when certain people slandered his beloved wife of adultery, (which she was totally free from) but he did not know which is why he spent a whole month in worry. If he was the knower of the unseen, he surely would have said it was lies. We as Muslims should believe that our beloved Prophet Muhammad ﷺ knew the knowledge of the unseen more than anyone on the surface of the earth, but only what Allāh ﷻ has allowed. It is only Allāh ﷻ Who has full knowledge regarding all matters, including the unseen.

Science of Dreams

إِذْ قَالَ يُوسُفُ لِأَبِيهِ يَا أَبَتِ إِنِّي رَأَيْتُ أَحَدَ عَشَرَ كَوْكَبًا وَّالشَّمْسَ وَالْقَمَرَ رَأَيْتُهُمْ لِي سَاجِدِيْنَ

[4] When Yūsuf said to his father, "O my beloved father, indeed I have seen eleven stars and the sun and the moon, I have seen them prostrating to me."

Subḥān-Allāh, Sayyidunā Yūsuf عليه السلام was just a young boy at the time but look at the respect he had for his father. In Arabic, يَاأَبِيْ means 'my father' and Sayyidunā Yūsuf عليه السلام says يَاأَبَتِ which means, 'O my beloved, respected father'. In the same way, Sayyidunā Ibrāhīm عليه السلام addressed his father Āzar:

إِذْ قَالَ لِأَبِيهِ يَا أَبَتِ لِمَ تَعْبُدُ مَا لَا يَسْمَعُ وَلَا يُبْصِرُ وَلَا يُغْنِي عَنْكَ شَيْئًا

(Mention) when he said to his father, "O my beloved father, why do you worship that which does not hear and does not see and will not benefit you at all?"(19:42).

Even though Āzar was a disbeliever, lets observe the respect. Unfortunately, many people do not give an ounce of that respect to their believing fathers, who have done so much for them.

Allāh ﷻ tells us in this verse exactly how Sayyidunā Yūsuf عليه السلام related his dream to his father, Sayyidunā Ya'qūb عليه السلام. As mentioned earlier, Sayyidunā Yūsuf عليه السلام was a young boy at the time, hence he is speaking in a manner in which children speak. Sayyidunā Yūsuf عليه السلام narrates that he saw eleven stars, the sun and the moon and he saw them prostrating to him. This repetition is customary in the speech of children.

As Sayyidunā Yūsuf عليه السلام matures into an adult, he becomes famous in the field of dream interpretation. This is why he praises Allāh ﷻ for teaching him this special knowledge in the 101th verse. Dream interpretation is a science in itself. A person may see something that is (apparently) very bad, when in actual fact, it has a very good meaning and result. Vice versa, a person may see something they perceive as very good when in reality it is very bad.

A person went to Imām Ibn Sīrīn ﷻ, the Imām of dream interpretation, telling him that he saw his house getting burnt down in his dream. Imām Sāhib told him to dig in the room in which he saw the fire and he will find treasure. So that is exactly what the man did, and he was correct. Imām Sāhib became well known in terms of his dream interpretation and sometime afterwards, another person saw a similar dream. This person became joyous and excited, thinking he was about to become rich. Instead, Imām Sāhib told him to quickly run and save his family because there was an actual fire in his home! People became confused and questioned the Imām Sāhib about the difference of both dreams. Imām Sāhib mentioned how the first person who saw the dream, did so in the winter time. In the winter season, if you see heat or fire, it is a good sign. However, if you see heat in the summer time, which is when the second person saw their dream, this is dangerous as heat plus heat is dangerous.

Accordingly, when interpreting dreams there are various factors to consider. A person's name, the time they saw their dream, the month and who they saw in their dream if they saw a person etc. If a person sees somebody called Bashīr or Bushrā, this means glad tidings. In contrast, if a person sees somebody called Nazīr, there is some indication of warning. If somebody named Suhail, Sahl or Sahla is seen, then this will mean that a matter will become easy. Every name has an effect.

Also, some dreams can come true but in later years. A prime example is when the Holy Prophet ﷺ saw a dream that he would go to Makkah to perform the pilgrimage, but, this didn't come true at that moment in time. The Holy Prophet ﷺ and the Sahābah ؆ were prevented from entering Makkah, and were told to come the following year, which is what happened.

قَالَ يَا بُنَيَّ لَا تَقْصُصْ رُؤْيَاكَ عَلَى إِخْوَتِكَ فَيَكِيدُوا لَكَ كَيْدًا ۖ إِنَّ الشَّيْطَانَ لِلْإِنْسَانِ عَدُوٌّ مُّبِينٌ

[5] He said (Sayyidunā Ya'qūb) "O my beloved son, do not mention this dream to your brothers, so they will conspire/plot against you. Indeed Shaytān is an open enemy for the human beings.

Sayyidunā Ya'qūb ﷺ instantly understood the dream as he was not a normal person, he was a Prophet of Allāh ﷻ. He immediately understood that the eleven stars were referring to Sayyidunā Yūsuf's ﷺ brothers (whom were eleven) and the sun and the moon referred to himself and his wife, the mother of Sayyidunā Yūsuf ﷺ.

Sajdah (prostration) was seen as a sign of respect in the earlier historical periods, it was known as Sajdah Ta'zīm (prostration for respect). However, later it was made forbidden in Islām. So, Sayyidunā Ya'qūb ﷺ realised that if Sayyidunā Yūsuf ﷺ was to narrate this to his brothers, they would understand the element of respect in the dream and as a result, become jealous of their brother.

Speciality of Sayyidunā Yūsuf ﷺ

وَكَذٰلِكَ يَجْتَبِيْكَ رَبُّكَ وَيُعَلِّمُكَ مِنْ تَأْوِيْلِ الْأَحَادِيْثِ وَيُتِمُّ نِعْمَتَهٗ عَلَيْكَ وَعَلٰى اٰلِ يَعْقُوْبَ كَمَا أَتَمَّهَا عَلٰى أَبَوَيْكَ مِنْ قَبْلُ إِبْرَاهِيْمَ وَإِسْحَاقَ ۚ إِنَّ رَبَّكَ عَلِيْمٌ حَكِيْمٌ

[6] And in this way your Lord has chosen you and He has taught you the meaning of dreams and He will fulfill His blessings upon you and upon the family of Ya'qūb like the way He has completed upon both your fathers before that, Ibrāhīm and Ishāq. Indeed your Lord is the One Who is the Most Knowledgeable, the Most Wise."

Sayyidunā Ya'qūb ﷺ is telling his son that Allāh ﷻ has truly chosen him. Allāh ﷻ selected Sayyidunā Yūsuf ﷺ because of his magnificence and high status.

Once a person asked the Holy Prophet ﷺ, "مَنْ أَكْرَمُ النَّاسِ؟" (Who is the most noble of the people?). The Holy Prophet ﷺ gave a very beautiful response. He said,

اَلْكَرِيْمُ ابْنُ الْكَرِيْمِ ابْنِ الْكَرِيْمِ ابْنِ الْكَرِيْمِ. يُوْسُفُ ابْنُ يَعْقُوْبَ ابْنِ اِسْحَاقَ ابْنِ اِبْرَاهِيْمَ.

"The most noble is the son of the noble (who is) the son of the noble (who is) the son of the noble." This refers to Yūsuf Ibn Ya'qūb Ibn Ishāq Ibn Ibrāhīm ﷺ. Sayyidunā Yūsuf ﷺ, his father Sayyidunā Ya'qūb ﷺ, his grandfather Sayyidunā Ishāq ﷺ and his great

17

grandfather, Sayyidunā Ibrāhīm عليه السلام were all prophets. And it is Sayyidunā Yūsuf عليه السلام who is the *most* noble. So, the speciality of Sayyidunā Yūsuf عليه السلام is that besides him, there are no other prophets who have four genealogies (generations) who are prophets.

So, Allāh سبحانه وتعالى is informing us in this verse that He has chosen Sayyidunā Yūsuf عليه السلام for prophethood. This was forecasted by the dream Sayyidunā Yūsuf عليه السلام saw in regards to the eleven stars, the sun and the moon prostrating to him. The aspect of prostration is interpreted as the manifestation of respect. Hence, this dream informs us that Sayyidunā Yūsuf عليه السلام will reach a stage where his family will surely respect him. The mention of 'prostration' does not necessarily mean in the literal sense.

Allāh سبحانه وتعالى also mentions here how He has taught Sayyidunā Yūsuf عليه السلام the intricacies behind dream interpretation, which is another blessing. Not everybody can interpret dreams, it is a lot harder than people perceive.

The word ni'mah (blessing) is referring to prophethood. Surely, the bestowment and honour of prophethood is one of the biggest blessings a person could achieve. From the family of Sayyidunā Ya'qūb عليه السلام, all the way till Sayyidunā Īsā عليه السلام, all the Prophets were from Banū Isrāīl—this is how Allāh سبحانه وتعالى fulfilled the blessings over these Prophets عليهم السلام. 'Isrāīl' is another name for Sayyidunā Ya'qūb عليه السلام. The word 'Isrāīl' means Abdullah. 'Isrā' means 'abd' (servant), 'īl' refers to Allāh ﷻ and 'banū' means sons. Therefore 'Banū Isrāīl means the sons of Ya'qūb (who is a servant of Allāh ﷻ).

Allāh ﷻ also mentions how He favoured Sayyidunā Ibrāhīm ﷺ. Subhān-Allāh, Allāh ﷻ made him Khalīl (friend). Moreover, Khalīl does not mean a normal friend, it means a very close friend.

Wisdom of Allāh ﷻ

Then the verse is concluded by, **Indeed your Lord is the All Knowing, the Most Wise.**

Allāh ﷻ knows what He is doing, He is Alīm and He does whatever He wishes according to His sublime wisdom. Allāh's ﷻ divine wisdom surpasses any 'logical' reasoning we humans may possess. Considering this, just because we do not immediately get something the moment we pray and ask Allāh ﷻ for, this does not mean that Allāh ﷻ is not answering our prayer. He may be answering it in a way that is better and more fulfilling for us, we just don't realise. There is also wisdom behind Allāh's ﷻ withholding of answering our Du'ās. This abstinence will be better for us, as everything is playing its part according to the greater plan that Allāh ﷻ has.

In terms of the context then, we can understand why Allāh ﷻ may not give something straight away. So Sayyidunā Yūsuf ﷺ should not worry, his respect and reuniting of family will come at a time known to Allāh ﷻ. Other occurrences need to happen before this pinnacle moment.

However, this does not mean that we don't work hard, and just idly expect things to happen. One of the distinct messages we learn from the story of Sayyidunā Yūsuf عليه السلام is that we must work hard. Just by observing the difficulties that Sayyidunā Yūsuf عليه السلام faced; his brothers becoming jealous and envious towards him, resulting in them throwing him in the well, then being sold as a slave, working for Zulaikha, dealing with wrongful slander, going to prison etc. Allāh ﷻ raised his rank because of all these struggles and perseverance.

لَقَدْ كَانَ فِيْ يُوْسُفَ وَإِخْوَتِه آيَاتٌ لِّلسَّائِلِيْنَ

[7] Indeed in Yūsuf and his brothers, there are signs for those people who are asking questions.

The noble story of Sayyidunā Yūsuf عليه السلام is not a mere fairy-tale of Zulaikha falling in love, there are so many signs, Masā'il, eyeopeners and reminders embedded within each unique stage of his life. Allāh ﷻ mentions the word 'Āyāt,' the plural form of 'āyah' (sign), meaning there are so many signs for those inquisitive people, who have a sweet zeal for knowledge. For these kinds of people, there are plenty of signs that will answer any questions they may have.

Jealousy of the Brothers

إِذْ قَالُوا لَيُوسُفُ وَأَخُوهُ أَحَبُّ إِلَىٰ أَبِينَا مِنَّا وَنَحْنُ عُصْبَةٌ إِنَّ أَبَانَا لَفِي ضَلَالٍ مُّبِينٍ

**[8] When they said, "Indeed Yūsuf and his brother are more be-
loved to our father than us, and we are a strong group. Indeed
our father is on clear misguidance.**

Now the story starts to unravel, starting with the envy and spite the
eleven brothers had towards Sayyidunā Yūsuf عليه السلام and the youngest
brother– Binyāmīn (Benjamin). This verse describes to us the scene
when the brothers got together and started to incite these statements
about their younger brothers, Yūsuf and Binyāmīn, who were from
another mother.

The elder brothers could not understand the reason for this. They
would think, surely *we* should be more beloved because we are a big,
strong group of brothers. We can bring so much benefit to our father, we can carry out any work that needs doing, go to the market
place, cut a tree, work on the fields and so on, but these younger
brothers of ours do nothing but sit and talk with our father. Why is it
that they are more beloved when they don't bring real benefit the
way we do? The brothers found this issue quite strange and unusual.

They found it that strange that they believed their father to be in
clear error. Thus, he is apparently making a manifest mistake because
logically, he should have thought that the elder brothers are going to

help whenever needed. So this was the Mashwara (consultation) the
brothers were doing.

Despicable Plot

اقْتُلُوْا يُوْسُفَ أَوِ اطْرَحُوهُ أَرْضًا يَّخْلُ لَكُمْ وَجْهُ أَبِيْكُمْ وَتَكُوْنُوْا مِنْ بَعْدِهٖ قَوْمًا صَالِحِيْنَ

**[9] Kill Yūsuf or throw him into a land, so for you your father's
attention will be free and then be after this, righteous people.**

Now, their jealousy, enmity, malice and spite reached such an extent
to which they started plotting to remove their brother, Sayyidunā
Yūsuf ﷺ. Furthermore, the jealousy intensified when Sayyidunā
Yūsuf ﷺ, due to young age and naivety disclosed the dream to his
brothers. Firstly, they saw Yūsuf ﷺ as the problem that they had to
deal with, and to deal with him efficiently they needed to get rid of
him. So the idea was put forward of killing him. Following this, one
of the ten brothers, Yahūda (Jūda) disagreed. He had that sense of
conscience in him and could not imagine to see his own blood
brother being killed. And as a result, he proposed a different plan.
He agreed with the objective of getting rid of Yūsuf ﷺ but recognized that there are many ways to do this, and they would not have
to resort to something as brutal as killing.

Sayyidunā Yūsuf ﷺ should be thrown into a far land and in that
way, Sayyidunā Ya'qūb ﷺ will have no choice but to turn to the rest
of the brothers. As there will be no Yūsuf, father's attention will be-

come sincerely for us – this was their reasoning, and of course, it was complemented by Shaytān's help.

Devil's Deception

When we look at the end of this verse, we encounter one of Shaytān's traps upon mankind. The brothers plotting of killing Sayyidunā Yūsuf عليه السلام or shunning him to a far land, is clearly a major sin and they acknowledged this. Pay attention at the way Shaytān made them overlook and justify their ideas 'Be pious people after-wards'. Meaning, carry out the sin, get rid of Yūsuf عليه السلام, then feel re-morse and repent to Allāh ﷻ. After this you'll be good.

Shaytān works on different people in different ways. For the student of knowledge, a big misconception is that after they graduate from their Ālim course, they will then become pious, righteous and saintly individual. When in actual fact, this is false. The habits that are in-stilled within a student during their years of studying will determine their actions post-graduation. If the student spends time implement-ing their knowledge, leaving bad habits and forming new, praisewor-thy ones, then Subhān-Allāh this is excellent. However, if the student doesn't instil good actions in their years of studying and are still ha-bitual in disliked or sinful acts, even *if* they graduate, they will be the same. There are so many advices from scholars and saints regarding the etiquettes of learning, and a clear theme that is consistent amongst them is the need to work hard and spiritually cleanse one-self, to gain 'ilm in the correct manner.

The Story

قَالَ قَائِلٌ مِّنْهُمْ لَا تَقْتُلُوا يُوسُفَ وَأَلْقُوهُ فِي غَيَابَتِ الْجُبِّ يَلْتَقِطْهُ بَعْضُ السَّيَّارَةِ إِن كُنتُمْ فَاعِلِينَ

[10] One person from them said, "Don't kill Yūsuf, throw him into the darkness of the well. Some travellers will pick him up, if you really want to do that."

Yahūda is the speaker referred to here. Previously when he put forth the idea of throwing Sayyidunā Yūsuf ﷺ into another land, he received backlash because Sayyidunā Yūsuf ﷺ might follow them and come back. So then he raised the idea of throwing him into a well. As Yūsuf ﷺ will not be able to climb out of it, he can only wait for travellers to come in search for water and then they would take him somewhere.

So, after this consultation all they had to do was speak to their father. This was the hardest part. They decided to appoint a spokesman amongst them who would speak properly, refraining from any mistakes.

قَالُوا يَا أَبَانَا مَا لَكَ لَا تَأْمَنَّا عَلَىٰ يُوسُفَ وَإِنَّا لَهُ لَنَاصِحُونَ

[11] They said, "O our father, what is wrong that you don't trust us regarding Yūsuf, and indeed we are for him very good advisors."

The brothers would plead with Sayyidunā Ya'qūb ﷵ. Why don't you trust us? Do you think we are going to kill him or cause trouble to him? He is our brother at the end of the day, from the same father. Even though our mothers are different, we are still from the same father. Yūsuf ﷵ always stays at home with you, but we want to take him out with us, we're having a picnic. We won't take Binyāmīn because he's very young, so instead we'll take Yūsuf ﷵ.

أَرْسِلْهُ مَعَنَا غَدًا يَّرْتَعْ وَيَلْعَبْ وَإِنَّا لَهُ لَحَافِظُونَ

[12] Send him with us tomorrow, he will benefit and play, and indeed we will safeguard him."

The word يَرْتَعْ means 'to benefit'. The scholars have said, over here it refers to eating (picnic) and enjoying oneself.

قَالَ إِنِّي لَيَحْزُنُنِي أَن تَذْهَبُوا بِهِ وَأَخَافُ أَن يَّأْكُلَهُ الذِّئْبُ وَأَنتُمْ عَنْهُ غَافِلُونَ

[13] (Ya'qūb) said, "Indeed it grieves me that you take him away and I fear that the wolf will eat him and you will be completely heedless."

25

Sayyidunā Ya'qūb's ﷺ reasoning is very accurate. Many times people will be given a responsibility but they don't see to it accordingly.
As a result, something goes wrong, sometimes catastrophically
wrong. When these tragic things happen and the person responsible
is asked, "Where were you?" it appeared they were busy with some
other matter, neglecting their responsibility or not being aware
enough.

قَالُوا لَئِنْ أَكَلَهُ الذِّئْبُ وَنَحْنُ عُصْبَةٌ إِنَّا إِذًا لَّخَاسِرُونَ

**[14] They said, "If the wolf eats him, and we are a big group, in-
deed we are complete losers."**

فَلَمَّا ذَهَبُوا بِهِ وَأَجْمَعُوا أَن يَجْعَلُوهُ فِي غَيَابَتِ الْجُبِّ ۚ وَأَوْحَيْنَا إِلَيْهِ لَتُنَبِّئَنَّهُم بِأَمْرِهِمْ هَٰذَا
وَهُمْ لَا يَشْعُرُونَ

**[15] When they took him away and they made firm intention
that they would put him in the darkness of the well, and We revealed towards him that surely you will inform them regarding
the matter (this matter of theirs) and they will not realise.**

The use of the word 'revealed' here, does not mean revelation—
because he was not a prophet yet. Rather, Allāh ﷻ put in Sayyidunā
Yūsuf's ﷺ heart that, a time will come in the future when, this
matter that they're doing now (putting him in the well) will come up

again. You'll remind them of it in the future, and they will not recognise you.

In the same way Allāh ﷻ inspired the bumble bee in Sūrah Nahl and the mother of Sayyidunā Mūsā عليه السلام, He inspired this thought into Sayyidunā Yūsuf's عليه السلام heart. It is divine inspiration, not Wahī.

وَجَاءُوْۤا اَبَاهُمْ عِشَاءً يَّبْكُوْنَ

[16] And they came to their father at night, crying.

The brothers could have come back to Sayyidunā Ya'qūb عليه السلام in the daytime but they chose not to. The sheer shame they had for lying to their parents in the daytime prevented them from confronting their father face to face. Thus, they thought it would be better to come when it would be dark whilst pretending to cry.

قَالُوْا يَاۤ اَبَانَاۤ اِنَّا ذَهَبْنَا نَسْتَبِقُ وَتَرَكْنَا يُوْسُفَ عِنْدَ مَتَاعِنَا فَاَكَلَهُ الذِّئْبُ ۚ وَمَاۤ اَنْتَ بِمُؤْمِنٍ لَّنَا وَلَوْ كُنَّا صَادِقِيْنَ

[17] They said, "O our beloved father, indeed we went racing and we left Yūsuf in the presence of our goods so a wolf ate him, and you will not be believing us even though we are telling the truth."

The brothers made up a tale of them leaving Sayyidunā Yūsuf عَلَيْهِ السَّلَام with their belongings, bags and picnic items whilst they were running and so a wolf killed and devoured him.

Just by the speech of the brothers it is plain to see how untruthful they are being. It is universally common, especially amongst children to try to cover up their naughtiness or lie, by negating it themselves before their parents do. When a child says, 'Mum you won't believe me but…' or 'You'll think I'm lying…' etc., it is usually a defence mechanism to protect themselves. Interestingly, the parents know what's going on, because they have spent a lifetime going through the same thing so they are not easily outsmarted.

Likewise, when Sayyidunā Yūsuf's عَلَيْهِ السَّلَام brothers were saying to their father, Sayyidunā Ya'qūb عَلَيْهِ السَّلَام "you will not believe us even though we are telling the truth", this statement alone suggests they are lying.

وَجَاءُوا عَلٰى قَمِيْصِهٖ بِدَمٍ كَذِبٍۚ قَالَ بَلْ سَوَّلَتْ لَكُمْ أَنْفُسُكُمْ أَمْرًاۚ فَصَبْرٌ جَمِيْلٌؕ وَاللّٰهُ الْمُسْتَعَانُ عَلٰى مَا تَصِفُوْنَ

[18] They came upon his shirt with false blood. (Ya'qūb) said, "But your souls have beautified this for you, so patience is best. Allāh is the Helper upon what you are describing.

When the brothers came to Sayyidunā Ya'qūb عَلَيْهِ السَّلَام concealing the truth, they tried to make their lie convincing by presenting proof.

They killed a goat and smeared its blood upon a shirt and put this forward as being Sayyidunā Yūsuf's عليه السلام shirt that he wore when the wolf killed him. The thing about telling lies is, that they always seem to come out in the end. Liars always get caught in some way or the other. Sayyidunā Ya'qūb عليه السلام thought to himself – Subhān-Allāh, what a kind wolf! What a lovely and gentle wolf it was that politely asked Yūsuf عليه السلام to take off his shirt so that it could steadily devour him. Meaning, where are the rips in the shirt? Surely, if a wolf *had* eaten Sayyidunā Yūsuf عليه السلام, you would find more than a few drops of blood, you would see tears and rips to say the least. The shirt was not torn at all, hence, Sayyidunā Ya'qūb عليه السلام said their nafs (soul) had did this. More specifically, it was the Nafs-Ammārah.

There are three types of Nafs:

1. Nafs Ammārah—soul that prompts towards evil.
2. Nafs Lawwāmah—soul that blames oneself.
3. Nafs Mutmainnah—soul that is content.

So, as a result of his sons plot and deception, Sayyidunā Ya'qūb عليه السلام responded by adopting beautiful patience. The only thing a person can do when he is afflicted, is be patient. The situation Sayyidunā Ya'qūb عليه السلام was placed in, called for patience.

Beauty in the Qur'ān

The word جَمِيْلٌ has come three times in the Qur'ān:

1. صبر جميل: 'Beautiful Patience' refers to that patience in where there is no complaint. Whatever happens, Alhamdulillāh! Usually when *we* go through something, we complain to everyone we know as if this will help our situation. Little do we realise that complaining to the creation is futile as it is Allāh ﷻ Who has the power to change all situations. And this is the patience that Sayyidunā Ya'qūb عليه السلام exercised.

2. صفح جميل: Safh-Jamīl refers to beautiful forgiveness. This is when a person forgives another person and never reminds them of it. After a fall out or a dispute, the person is quick to overlook the one in wrong and their friendship is rekindled as though nothing ever happened.

3. هجر جميل: Hajr-Jamīl refers to going away from someone whilst you are at good terms with that person. If you cannot get along with someone, before you depart from them ensure that you are on good terms with them. After you depart, do not mention anything bad about that person. A person that cannot see eye-to-eye with another, yet retains the greeting of Salām and does not backbite him, is practicing Hajr-Jamīl.

Love Requires Effort

Being a Nabi of Allāh ﷻ, Sayyidunā Ya'qūb عليه السلام had an inkling that there was something behind the brothers and their story, but at the same time, he realised that he was being tested by the Almighty Allāh ﷻ. He was such a prominent and righteous Prophet, and look at how much he was tested by Allāh ﷻ. This is what we need to re-member, Allāh ﷻ tests those whom He loves. Whenever you are afflicted with any kind of worry, harm, anxiety, stress, illness, dis-comfort or trouble, turn to Allāh ﷻ. Should you respond in the cor-rect way, i.e. to ask Allāh ﷻ for patience and exercise it, then you will be rewarded! Subhān-Allāh. Sayyidunā Ya'qūb عليه السلام was being tested by Allāh ﷻ, and as we continue to read through the story, we'll see how Allāh ﷻ tested both Prophets, Yūsuf and Ya'qūb عليه السلام.

If you love somebody, then you follow them as best as you can. This is a standard rule that everybody recognises. Once, a person said to our beloved Muhammad ﷺ, "I love you, O Messenger of Allāh ﷺ." The Prophet ﷺ told the person that if you love me, be prepared to go through hardship. The way that water trickles down a slope into a valley—just imagine that speed– poverty will come to you even fast-er than that.

Mother of the believers, Sayyidah Ā'isha رضي الله عنها stated, "One moon, two moons and three moons passed without the fire being lit in the house of the Prophet ﷺ". For up to three months they lived on water and dates Subhān-Allāh. Its easy to make the claim of loving the

Prophet ﷺ, but rather than mere lip service, we need to be ready for the hardships that are to come our way. If you really do love somebody, you need to have their good habits and traits within you. Hence, whilst going through afflictions such as poverty, we should remain grateful, cheerful and content, the way the Prophet ﷺ did.

In the latter part of the verse, Sayyidunā Ya'qūb عليه السلام teaches us some invaluable advice. He says, Allāh ﷻ is the One Whom we ask help from upon those things that you describe. Here, he means what the eleven brothers are describing of their brother being killed and devoured by a wolf. In other words, 'O Allāh, these people have done this and I'm asking for Your help'. This is how we need to approach our hardships of life. If you are having problems with your Nikāh, or in your studies, or at work, or within the family, whatever it may be, Shaytān is trying to overcome you so you must be firm, seek help from Allāh ﷻ and be patient.

Yūsuf عليه السلام is Sold

وَجَاءَتْ سَيَّارَةٌ فَأَرْسَلُوا وَارِدَهُمْ فَأَدْلَى دَلْوَهُ ۖ قَالَ يَا بُشْرَىٰ هٰذَا غُلَامٌ ۚ وَأَسَرُّوهُ بِضَاعَةً ۚ وَاللهُ عَلِيمٌ بِمَا يَعْمَلُونَ

[19] And the caravan (of the travellers) came, they sent their water-searcher and he dropped the bucket. He said, "O glad tidings, this is a child." And they hid him (the child) as a commodity. And Allāh knows those things that they do.

32

When the travellers of the caravan stopped and sent the person who is in charge of finding the water to seek out water, he was astonished to find a beautiful child in the well. The travellers thought to themselves that they would hide young Sayyidunā Yūsuf الـعـلـيـه and sell him for a big price. Allāh ﷻ knew all about their intentions and purpose of taking him.

وَشَرَوْهُ بِثَمَنٍ بَخْسٍ دَرَاهِمَ مَعْدُوْدَةٍ وَّكَانُوْا فِيْهِ مِنَ الزَّاهِدِيْنَ

[20] And they sold him for a cheap price - fixed dirhams- and they were regarding him (Yūsuf) reluctant.

After Sayyidunā Yūsuf's الـعـلـيـه brothers dropped him in the well, they moved to a side and patiently waited to see what would happen. As they saw the caravan arriving, they emerged and told the travellers that Yūsuf الـعـلـيـه was their slave, who ran away. Subḥān-Allāh, they actually acted as though their own brother was their slave. If that wasn't bad enough, they then offered to sell him to the travellers, who accepted. And how much did they sell him for? Some scholars say, 18 dirhams *only*.

From the ten brothers, all received two dirhams each except for Yahūda. Some say he was the eldest and the cleverest. He was the only one out of them that had love for Sayyidunā Yūsuf الـعـلـيـه hence, prevented his brothers from killing Sayyidunā Yūsuf الـعـلـيـه. He stated, "How can I possibly sell my brother, who is free and then take money? What an evil and inhumane thing to do." So nine of the brothers took their share and Yahūda refrained.

The reluctancy refers to the brothers wish of simply getting rid of him. They did not want any money at first, their motive was only to shun him away from the family so that Sayyidunā Ya'qūb عليه السلام could start paying *them* attention. So they were reluctant. And Yahūda, although it was evil to throw Yūsuf عليه السلام into the well and watch him being taken away by mere strangers, he was content knowing that he was alive. It was hard enough to convince the other nine brothers to not kill him so he was happy to see that Sayyidunā Yūsuf عليه السلام would be alive and well.

After this, the travellers went to the marketplace in Egypt and presented Yūsuf عليه السلام as a slave to be bought. Even as a young boy, his beauty was such that it drew in so many bids. Everybody wanted to buy him, and the bids kept on increasing until a price was reached which was too expensive for the normal folk to pay. The only person who could buy him was the governor of Egypt. And so he did.

وَقَالَ الَّذِي اشْتَرَاهُ مِن مِّصْرَ لِامْرَأَتِه أَكْرِمِي مَثْوَاهُ عَسَى أَن يَّنفَعَنَا أَوْ نَتَّخِذَهُ وَلَدًا وَكَذٰلِكَ مَكَّنَّا لِيُوسُفَ فِي الْأَرْضِ وَلِنُعَلِّمَهُ مِن تَأْوِيلِ الْأَحَادِيثِ وَاللهُ غَالِبٌ عَلَى أَمْرِه وَلٰكِنَّ أَكْثَرَ النَّاسِ لَا يَعْلَمُونَ

[21] And the one who purchased him in Egypt said to his wife, "Respect his abode, it is hoped that he will benefit us or we will make him as our child." And in this way, We gave authority to Yūsuf on the earth and so We could teach him the meaning of

dreams. And Allāh is dominant over His matter but majority of the people do not know.

After buying Sayyidunā Yūsuf الَعَلَيْهِ, the governor of Egypt took him to his wife, Zulaikha and told her to **respect his abode**. There are a few meanings of this. In essence, its means to do khidmat (service) of this boy and look after him well. However his 'abode' could mean:

1.   His position. In other words, keep Sayyidunā Yūsuf الَعَلَيْهِ in a high, respectable position and status.
2.   His bedroom. As he would be staying in the governor of Egypt's home, Zulaikha is being instructed to ensure Sayyidunā Yūsuf has all the amenities, facilities and essentials that a boy needs.

Māshā-Allāh, he really wanted to be hospitable and accommodating towards Sayyidunā Yūsuf الَعَلَيْهِ. *We* should be like this. Even the Arabic greeting -اهلا وسهلا ومرحبا- is such an encompassing indicator of fruitful hospitality. اهلا means 'family'. So by saying اهلا you are saying, "you are family, please come in." سهلا means, 'easy'. In other words, you're telling the visitor to feel easy here, in your home. Then finally, مرحبا is 'Greetings!', 'We are so happy you are here!'

The governor of Egypt told Zulaikha, '**It is hoped that he will benefit us.**' The governor could recognise that Sayyidunā Yūsuf الَعَلَيْهِ was intelligent and righteous, just by gazing upon him.

The Three that Recognised

The history books mention three people who recognised certain qualities of their colleagues. The first is the governor of Egypt. Just by *seeing* Sayyidunā Yūsuf ﵇, he said that he would bring benefit to them. The governor could see from his face the signs of piety and good character.

The second was the daughter of Sayyidunā Shuaib ﵇. She recognized the value of Sayyidunā Mūsā ﵇. After seeing Sayyidunā Mūsā ﵇ lifting the covering of the well, which usually takes ten people to lift, she immediately saw how strong he was. Then, whilst they were both walking back, Sayyidunā Mūsā ﵇ Māshā-Allāh, didn't try to speak to her or unnecessarily interact with her – this is how she recognized the worth, modesty and status of Sayyidunā Mūsā ﵇. This is why she asked her father, Sayyidunā Shuaib ﵇ to employ him as a worker, because he possessed both qualities; strength and trust.

The third was Sayyidunā Abū Bakr Siddīq ﵁. During his last moments, he chose Sayyidunā Umar ﵁ to become the Khalīfa after him. The people questioned his decision and asked, "Why would you appoint Sayyidunā Umar who is so strict and harsh?" They even commented, "What will you say to Allāh ﷻ regarding this. So, Sayyidunā Abū Bakr ﵁ said, "I will say to Allāh ﷻ that after me I have appointed the best person on the surface of earth." And it was true, he was the best person on earth in that moment of time.

Or we can make him our child:
Then the governor brought the idea of keeping Sayyidunā Yūsuf عليه السلام
as their own son. This was because him and Zulaikha had no children. So, he thought that maybe they could adopt Sayyidunā Yūsuf
عليه السلام.

And in this way, We gave authority to Yūsuf on the earth:
Allāh ﷻ is informing us that He blessed Sayyidunā Yūsuf عليه السلام with
authority and power. Despite the brothers plot of trying to get rid of
him and selling him as a slave, he lived in the house of the governor -
which had all types of bounties and luxuries. Sayyidunā Yūsuf عليه السلام
was living like a king already. Subhān-Allāh, he had every kind of
worldly entertainment he could have wanted, but, being the pious,
righteous slave of Allāh ﷻ that he was, he refrained.

And so We could teach him the meaning of dreams:
Allāh ﷻ gave Sayyidunā Yūsuf عليه السلام the special knowledge relating to
dreams. He blessed him with deep insight into this science, which is
not easy to learn. Dream interpretation comes from experience and
extensive knowledge of the Holy Qur'ān and Ahādīth. One can not
simply enroll on a course and expect to have gained this knowledge,
it is not as easy as that.

The final part of the verse reminds mankind that Allāh ﷻ is Dominant over His matter, but the majority of people do not know. Just
look at the crooked intentions the ten brothers had towards Sayyidunā Yūsuf عليه السلام. They wanted to eradicate him so they threw him

deep into the well, thinking that would work. But ultimately, whatever Allāh ﷻ wants to happen, will surely happen.

This is something we must always be aware of. If something is not written for you, you will never be able to get it. If Allāh ﷻ has written something for you, the whole world can go against it, but it will still happen nevertheless. We need to accept that Taqdīr (fate) is from Allāh ﷻ, whether good or bad. And Allāh ﷻ is the Most Wise.

وَلَمَّا بَلَغَ أَشُدَّهُ آتَيْنَاهُ حُكْمًا وَّعِلْمًا ۚ وَكَذٰلِكَ نَجْزِي الْمُحْسِنِينَ

[22] And when Yūsuf reached his youth, We gave him judgement and knowledge. And in this way We reward those people who carry out good deeds.

The word أَشُدَّ actually means 'strength'. Some scholars have stated that Allāh ﷻ is referring to actual strength whilst others believe that أَشُدَّ refers to Prophethood. In terms of the latter interpretation, Sayyidunā Yūsuf ﷺ reached the age of forty, and received Prophethood (just like all the other Ambiyā ﷺ). These days, we class a person to be old at the age of forty, when in reality, this is the age we are *supposed* to be strong. Unfortunately in todays' society, we tend to see a person being hit by numerous illnesses and conditions at the age of forty, which is quite contrary to the way it should be.

Allāh ﷻ is informing us that He gave Sayyidunā Yūsuf عليه السلام the ability to judge between people and also knowledge. Knowledge can refer to dream interpretation or Prophethood.

Significance of Good Deeds

Sayyidunā Yūsuf عليه السلام was from the 'Muhsinūn' (the doers of good). He was persistent in carrying out good deeds which is why, Allāh ﷻ is informing him and us, that He will definitely, without a doubt reward those who do good. Every single good deed you carry out, no matter how insignificant you think it is, there is always benefit. Allāh ﷻ is the best Rewarder and He will never leave any good deed unrewarded, Subhān-Allāh.

Allāh ﷻ even rewards the disbelievers if they have carried out good deeds!

Bukhāri and Muslim mention a detailed narration of when Abū Sufyān ؓ and Heraclius were talking about the Holy Prophet ﷺ. Heraclius asked him questions regarding the Holy Prophet ﷺ which Abū Sufyān answered truthfully. This account happened whilst Abū Sufyān was an enemy of the Holy Prophet ﷺ, yet he did not forge any lies or tales about him. When Heraclius asked him, 'Have you ever accused him of telling lies before his claim (to be a Prophet)?' Abū Sufyān replied, 'No.' (full account can be found in Bukhāri). It is said that because of Abū Sufyān's truthfulness, in the upcoming years he was guided by Allāh ﷻ to accept Islām and died as a Sahābi.

Abū Lahab was a clear, open enemy of Islām. Allāh ﷻ revealed a whole Sūrah on his account. The opening of Sūrah Lahab reads as follows:

تَبَّتْ يَدَا أَبِي لَهَبٍ وَتَبَّ

Destruction to the hands of Abū Lahab and let him be destroyed. (111:1)

Even this wretched man, who was disgraced by Allāh ﷻ and the people, was rewarded for *one* deed he performed. Allāhu-Akbar. When he received the news of his nephew being born (the Holy Prophet ﷺ) from his slave girl, he became so happy and good-willed that he immediately freed his slave girl by indicating with his finger. Abū Lahab's brother saw him in a dream and asked him what was wrong with him. He mentioned how he was going through so many hardships, but every Monday at a particular time Allāh ﷻ would give him ease. Then he explained how his nephew Muhammad ﷺ was born on a Monday, and that same finger he used to indicate the freeing of his slave girl- would spurt out a milky substance by the power of Allāh ﷻ. As soon as he would drink this, it would quench his thirst and he would have relief and ease for a moment. Subhān-Allāh, just because of this *one* deed, Allāh ﷻ rewarded him in such a profound way. Allāhu-Akbar! If this is the situation of a disbeliever who has been condemned to Hell by the Qur'ān, then what is the situation of a believer?

How can one belittle any good deed after reflecting on this?

Zulaikha's Plotting

وَرَاوَدَتْهُ الَّتِي هُوَ فِي بَيْتِهَا عَنْ نَّفْسِهِ وَغَلَّقَتِ الْأَبْوَابَ وَقَالَتْ هَيْتَ لَكَ ۚ قَالَ مَعَاذَ اللّٰهِ ۖ إِنَّهُ رَبِّي أَحْسَنَ مَثْوَايَ ۖ إِنَّهُ لَا يُفْلِحُ الظَّالِمُوْنَ

[23] And she, in whose house he was, sought to seduce him. She closed the doors and said, "Come, you." He said, "(I seek) the refuge of Allāh. Indeed, he is my master who has made good my residence. Indeed wrongdoers will not succeed."

Now, Allāh ﷻ mentions the story of Zulaikha and Sayyidunā Yūsuf عليه السلام. Zulaikha was the wife of the governor of Egypt. She was the very person who was told by the governor to look after Sayyidunā Yūsuf عليه السلام. Whilst Sayyidunā Yūsuf عليه السلام grew, so did his beauty and this matured handsome man was in the eye of Zulaikha now. She was obsessed and filled with love for Sayyidunā Yūsuf عليه السلام. The love she had for him dazzled her to such an extent, that she plotted against him.

The above verse depicts the scene when Zulaikha tried to seduce Sayyidunā Yūsuf عليه السلام. She had beautified herself especially for him and then locked all the doors. After calling him to the evil sin, Sayyidunā Yūsuf عليه السلام started to run away.

وَلَقَدْ هَمَّتْ بِهِ ۖ وَهَمَّ بِهَا لَوْلَا أَن رَّأَىٰ بُرْهَانَ رَبِّهِ ۚ كَذَٰلِكَ لِنَصْرِفَ عَنْهُ السُّوءَ وَالْفَحْشَاءَ ۚ إِنَّهُ مِنْ عِبَادِنَا الْمُخْلَصِينَ

[24] And indeed, she intended and he would have inclined if he had not seen the signs of his Lord. In this way We removed from him sins and immorality. Indeed he was amongst Our chosen servants.

Which man would be able to resist a beautiful woman, enticing him, except a God-fearing servant of Allāh ﷻ. Allāh ﷻ safeguarded Sayyidunā Yūsuf عليه السلام from the evil sin. It is in the nature of a Prophet that he can never commit a sin, either before prophethood or after, nor a major sin or a minor one.

وَاسْتَبَقَا الْبَابَ وَقَدَّتْ قَمِيصَهُ مِن دُبُرٍ وَأَلْفَيَا سَيِّدَهَا لَدَى الْبَابِ ۚ قَالَتْ مَا جَزَاءُ مَنْ أَرَادَ بِأَهْلِكَ سُوءًا إِلَّا أَن يُسْجَنَ أَوْ عَذَابٌ أَلِيمٌ

[25] Then both of them ran to the door and she tore his shirt from the back and they found her husband at the door. She said, "What is the punishment of the one who intends evil with your wife but that he be imprisoned or a painful punishment?"

When Sayyidunā Yūsuf ﷺ ran away from Zulaikha, she ran after him, trying to engage in the sin. Zulaikha grabbed Sayyidunā Yūsuf's ﷺ shirt from behind. The governor of Egypt (Zulaikha's husband) was at the door which is when she framed Sayyidunā Yūsuf ﷺ. She unlawfully accused Sayyidunā Yūsuf الالَّيِّلِا, then demanded that he be punished!

The Young Witness

قَالَ هِيَ رَاوَدَتْنِيْ عَن نَّفْسِيْ ۚ وَشَهِدَ شَاهِدٌ مِّنْ أَهْلِهَا إِن كَانَ قَمِيْصُهٗ قُدَّ مِنْ قُبُلٍ فَصَدَقَتْ وَهُوَ مِنَ الْكَاذِبِيْنَ

[26] He said, "It was she who sought to seduce me." And a witness from her family testified. "If his shirt is torn from the front, then she has told the truth, and he is of the liars.

وَإِنْ كَانَ قَمِيْصُهٗ قُدَّ مِنْ دُبُرٍ فَكَذَبَتْ وَهُوَ مِنَ الصَّادِقِيْنَ

[27] But if his shirt is torn from the back, then she has lied, and he is of the truthful."

Sayyidunā Yūsuf الالَّيِّلِا tried to explain his innocence. This is really important. If there is an allegation placed upon you wrongfully, you should try to clear the misconception.

The witness that Allāh ﷻ mentions refers to a young child that was unable to speak. Allāh ﷻ made him miraculously speak, to reveal the truth about Sayyidunā Yūsuf الالَّيِّلِا. Logically speaking, if Sayyidunā Yūsuf الالَّيِّلِا *was* the guilty party, he would have torn off his shirt, specifically the front of his shirt. It would be unlikely for a person in that moment to tear his shirt from the back. However for Zulaikha, who was trying to pursue Sayyidunā Yūsuf عليه السلام, it is very likely for her to tear the back of his shirt, as she had no access to the front side because he was running.

فَلَمَّا رَاٰی قَمِیۡصَہٗ قُدَّ مِنۡ دُبُرٍ قَالَ اِنَّہٗ مِنۡ کَیۡدِکُنَّ ؕ اِنَّ کَیۡدَکُنَّ عَظِیۡمٌ

[28] So when her husband saw his shirt torn from the back, he said, "Indeed, it is of the women's plan. Indeed your plan is great.

The governor of Egypt knew that Sayyidunā Yūsuf عليه السلام was innocent.

یُوۡسُفُ اَعۡرِضۡ عَنۡ ہٰذَا ٚ وَاسۡتَغۡفِرِیۡ لِذَنۡۢبِکِ ۚ اِنَّکِ کُنۡتِ مِنَ الۡخٰطِئِیۡنَ

[29] Yūsuf, ignore this. And (my wife), ask forgiveness for your sin. Indeed you were of the sinful."

Women Talk

وَقَالَ نِسْوَةٌ فِي الْمَدِينَةِ امْرَأَتُ الْعَزِيزِ تُرَاوِدُ فَتَاهَا عَن نَّفْسِهِ ۖ قَدْ شَغَفَهَا حُبًّا ۖ إِنَّا لَنَرَاهَا فِي ضَلَالٍ مُّبِينٍ

[30] And the females in the city said, "The wife of al-'Azīz is seeking to seduce her slave boy; he has impassioned her with love. Indeed, we see her (to be) in clear error."

The women in the city started to spread rumours about Zulaikha. They could not understand how a woman of her status and noble rank, could possibly fall in love with a slave. Being as beautiful as she was, she could have had anybody, but instead she wanted Sayyidunā Yūsuf السلام عليه. They realised that the love Zulaikha had for Sayyidunā Yūsuf السلام عليه had infatuated and fully overpowered her. Zulaikha remained firm and would tell them how they are only saying this because they have not seen him. She was so sure that once the women see Sayyidunā Yūsuf السلام عليه for themselves, they would realise why she is so in love with him.

Subhān-Allāh, the way Allāh ﷻ talks about Zulaikha is with such kindness. Unlike the women who spread these rumours, Allāh ﷻ screens her identity within the Qur'ān. He doesn't mention her name but rather, He makes reference to 'the wife of Azīz Misr'.

فَلَمَّا سَمِعَتْ بِمَكْرِهِنَّ أَرْسَلَتْ إِلَيْهِنَّ وَأَعْتَدَتْ لَهُنَّ مُتَّكَأً وَّآتَتْ كُلَّ وَاحِدَةٍ مِّنْهُنَّ سِكِّيْنًا وَّقَالَتِ اخْرُجْ عَلَيْهِنَّ ۖ فَلَمَّا رَأَيْنَهٗ أَكْبَرْنَهٗ وَقَطَّعْنَ أَيْدِيَهُنَّ وَقُلْنَ حَاشَ لِلّٰهِ مَا هٰذَا بَشَرًا إِنْ هٰذَا إِلَّا مَلَكٌ كَرِيْمٌ

[31] When she heard of their conspiracy, she sent a message towards them and prepared for them a sitting and she gave every one of them a knife. And she said, "Come out infront of them." When they saw him, they were amazed and they cut their hands. And they said, "Perfect is Allāh! He is not a human being. He is none but a very noble angel."

The women who were making allegations against Zulaikha were summoned by her for a gathering. In those days, there were no text messages or media, so Zulaikha, being the noble aristocratic woman she was, had an ambassador to deliver the message to the women. She gave each of them a knife and they started to cut different fruits. As this was happening, she called Sayyidunā Yūsuf ﷺ into the room. As soon as their eyes fell upon Sayyidunā Yūsuf ﷺ, they started to cut their hands and didn't even realise! They were so mesmerised by the immense beauty of Sayyidunā Yūsuf ﷺ, they were oblivious to the fact they had sharp knives in their hands. They believed him to be an angel.

Beauty of the Prophets ﷺ

There are two types of beauty. One is Sabāhat and the other is Malāhat:

Sabāhat is that beauty that when you see it, you become so dazzled, mesmerized and amazed. This is the beauty of Sayyidunā Yūsuf عليه السلام. As soon as the women saw him, instantly they were astounded. This is why some people choose to keep the name 'Sabīha' because of its' beautiful meaning.

Malāhat is that beauty which increases gradually. Whenever somebody looks at something, they are dazzled, but when they look at it again, it becomes more beautiful. This is the beauty of our noble Prophet Muhammad ﷺ. The Sahābah ؓ would be in awe whenever they gazed upon him.

Subhān-Allāh, there is a very warm and comforting truth for us Muslims. When a person enters Paradise, they will have the beauty of Sayyidunā Yūsuf عليه السلام, the voice of Sayyidunā Dāwūd عليه السلام, the height of Sayyidunā Ādam عليه السلام, the strength of Sayyidunā Mūsā عليه السلام, the kingdom of Sayyidunā Sulaimān عليه السلام and last but certainly not least, the noble character of Sayyidunā Muhammad ﷺ. A person will have all of these different qualities and specialities of the noble Ambiyā (Prophets) عليهم السلام. May Allāh ﷻ make us among them. Āmīn!

Yūsuf عليه السلام is Thrown in Prison

قَالَتْ فَذٰلِكُنَّ الَّذِي لُمْتُنَّنِي فِيهِ ۖ وَلَقَدْ رَاوَدتُّهُ عَن نَّفْسِهِ فَاسْتَعْصَمَ ۖ وَلَئِن لَّمْ يَفْعَلْ مَا
آمُرُهُ لَيُسْجَنَنَّ وَلَيَكُونًا مِّنَ الصَّاغِرِينَ

**[32] She said, "This is regarding which you are blaming me.
And yes I tried to seduce him regarding himself but he saved
himself. And if he doesn't do the thing that I order him to do, he
will surely be prisoned and surely he'll be from the disgraceful
people."**

Zulaikha may have admitted the truth but she doesn't stop there.
She threatens Sayyidunā Yūsuf عليه السلام that if he refuses again, she will
disgrace him by imprisoning him.

Sayyidunā Yūsuf عليه السلام replies by saying:

قَالَ رَبِّ السِّجْنُ أَحَبُّ إِلَيَّ مِمَّا يَدْعُونَنِي إِلَيْهِ ۖ وَإِلَّا تَصْرِفْ عَنِّي كَيْدَهُنَّ أَصْبُ إِلَيْهِنَّ وَأَكُن
مِّنَ الْجَاهِلِينَ

**[33] He said, "O my Lord, the prison is more beloved to me
than that which they are calling me towards." And if You do
not turn their conspiracy from me, I might incline towards
them and (thus) be of the ignorant."**

48

Sayyidunā Yūsuf عليه السلام made Duʿā to Allāh with such humbleness. He asks Allāh to save him from their planning, lest he begins to incline. This is a noble trait amongst the Prophets of Allāh, they never depended upon their piety. Rather, they would always ask Allāh to help them.

فَاسْتَجَابَ لَهُ رَبُّهُ فَصَرَفَ عَنْهُ كَيْدَهُنَّ ۚ إِنَّهُ هُوَ السَّمِيعُ الْعَلِيمُ

[35] So his Lord accepted his Duʿā, He turned away from him their conspiracy. Indeed He is the One Who listens and knows.

ثُمَّ بَدَا لَهُمْ مِنْ بَعْدِ مَا رَأَوُا الْآيَاتِ لَيَسْجُنُنَّهُ حَتَّىٰ حِينٍ

[35] Then it became apparent for them after what they saw of the signs that Azīz Misr should imprison him for a time.

The governor thought the best thing to do would be to imprison Sayyidunā Yūsuf عليه السلام for some time to help the situation. At this time, insults were being hurled at Zulaikha and there was much talk in the markets. If Sayyidunā Yūsuf عليه السلام was present this would only exacerbate things. So to calm down the situation, the governor decided to put Sayyidunā Yūsuf عليه السلام in prison. He remained in prison for nine years.

Ask Allāh 🕮 for Goodness

The scholars of Tafsīr inform us that if Sayyidunā Yūsuf عليه السلام had asked Allāh 🕮 for safety rather than prison, Allāh 🕮 would have given him that. But he prayed for prison and that is why it was accepted.

Many people make very explicit Du'ās unnecessarily. Sometime parents make Du'ās such as "O' Allāh give me this illness and let my son/daughter live." Such Du'ās should be avoided. We should make positive and optimistic Du'ās and ask Allāh 🕮 for safety. Nothing is hard for Allāh 🕮.

وَدَخَلَ مَعَهُ السِّجْنَ فَتَيَانِ ۖ قَالَ أَحَدُهُمَا إِنِّي أَرَانِي أَعْصِرُ خَمْرًا ۖ وَقَالَ الْآخَرُ إِنِّي أَرَانِي أَحْمِلُ فَوْقَ رَأْسِي خُبْزًا تَأْكُلُ الطَّيْرُ مِنْهُ ۖ نَبِّئْنَا بِتَأْوِيلِهِ ۖ إِنَّا نَرَاكَ مِنَ الْمُحْسِنِينَ

[36] And with him in the prison two youngsters entered. One of them said, "Indeed I saw myself squeezing wine and the other said, "Indeed I saw myself carrying bread on my head and the birds were eating from it. Inform us of its interpretation. Indeed we see you from those who do good."

Two youngsters approached Sayyidunā Yūsuf عليه السلام in the prison. One may ask, what made them approach him? At that time, he hadn't been present in the prison for that long. The answer is, his Akhlāq (manners). Sayyidunā Yūsuf عليه السلام made such a positive impression upon them by his good character and amazing conduct, they immediately inclined towards him. Just from his outward character they were able to recognise his nobility and righteousness.

We should follow the example of Sayyidunā Yūsuf ﷺ and perfect our character. If we were to do this, people would flock into Islām.

Wine is a Covering

The first youngster mentions how he saw himself in a dream, using different fruits to make wine. The word Khamr, literally means to cover. You may be thinking, what is the correlation between wine and covering? Wine and other forms of alcohol cover a person's intellect. When a person is drunk, his intelligence and sense of reality is distorted.

A Bedouin was once asked, هَلْ اَنْتَ تَشْرَبُ الْخَمْرَ؟ "Do you drink wine?" The Bedouin gave a beautiful response,

كَيْفَ اَشْرَبُ مَا يَشْرَبُ عَقْلِيْ؟ "How can I drink something which drinks my intelligence?" Subhan-Allāh. And it is very true. Intellect is the speciality that makes mankind the best of creation. Allāh ﷻ says:

لَقَدْ خَلَقْنَا الْإِنْسَانَ فِيْ أَحْسَنِ تَقْوِيْمٍ

Indeed We have created man in the best of stature. (95:4)

ثُمَّ رَدَدْنَاهُ أَسْفَلَ سَافِلِيْنَ

Then We returned him to the lowest of the low. (95:5)

Da'wah in Prison

قَالَ لَا يَأْتِيكُمَا طَعَامٌ تُرْزَقَانِهِ إِلَّا نَبَّأْتُكُمَا بِتَأْوِيلِهِ قَبْلَ أَنْ يَأْتِيَكُمَا ۚ ذَٰلِكُمَا مِمَّا عَلَّمَنِي رَبِّيْ
إِنِّيْ تَرَكْتُ مِلَّةَ قَوْمٍ لَّا يُؤْمِنُوْنَ بِاللهِ وَهُمْ بِالْآخِرَةِ هُمْ كَافِرُوْنَ

**He said, "The food will not come to you, which you will be fed,
but I will inform you both of the meaning before your food
comes to you. These are things which my Lord has taught me.
Indeed I have left the religion of the people who don't believe in
Allāh and regarding the Hereafter they are disbelievers.**

Sayyidunā Yūsuf ﷺ seized the opportunity of giving Da'wah here, which can be applied widely to different situations. To illustrate with an example, imagine a child begs their father for a sweet. In this moment when they are asking their father, their primary focus is that sweet, and nothing will take their mind off it. If the father was to advise the child in this moment, it would be completely useless because that advice will not resonate with them. Their mind is preoccupied thinking about the sweet. However, if the father tells the child that he will give them the sweet and perhaps shows them it, *then* says, "I need to tell you something important before I give you this sweet, so listen up", that child will listen attentively because they have been assured by the father that they'll receive the sweet.

In the same way, Sayyidunā Yūsuf ﷺ first tells the youngsters, "I will tell you the meaning of the dream before the food comes to you." Already, he has reassured the youngsters that their dreams will be interpreted. Now they will be thinking, Sayyidunā Yūsuf ﷺ has done this favour for us, we should listen to what he has to say. Once the youngsters start to listen, Sayyidunā Yūsuf ﷺ informs them about Tawhīd (Oneness of Allāh) and Islām. These people were idol worshippers, so this message had to be conveyed to them.

Sayyidunā Yūsuf ﷺ sought out a way to give Da'wah and spread the divine message of Islām. And we should adopt the same approach. As a teacher, parent, role-model, student etc. we should take up opportunities to give Da'wah. This excellent method is supported by Shaykh Abul-Hasan an-Nadwi ﷺ (author of Qasas un-Nabiyyīn). He states that when a person is in need of advice, their heart becomes very soft and more accepting. It begins to accept the advice the way a sponge absorbs water.

وَاتَّبَعْتُ مِلَّةَ آبَائِي إِبْرَاهِيمَ وَإِسْحَاقَ وَيَعْقُوبَ ۚ مَا كَانَ لَنَا أَنْ نُشْرِكَ بِاللّٰهِ مِنْ شَيْءٍ ۚ ذٰلِكَ مِنْ فَضْلِ اللّٰهِ عَلَيْنَا وَعَلَى النَّاسِ وَلٰكِنَّ أَكْثَرَ النَّاسِ لَا يَشْكُرُونَ

**I have followed the religion of my forefathers; Ibrāhim and
Ishāq and Ya'qūb. It is not for us that we ascribe partners to
Allāh. This is the grace of Allāh upon us and upon the people
but majority of the people are not grateful.**

After Sayyidunā Yūsuf ﷺ mentions how he left the religion of the
people in the previous verse, now he tells us what he follows. By following the religion of his forefathers, Allāh ﷻ made him successful.

$$يَا صَاحِبَيِ السِّجْنِ أَأَرْبَابٌ مُتَفَرِّقُونَ خَيْرٌ أَمِ اللهُ الْوَاحِدُ الْقَهَّارُ$$

**[38] O the two companions of the prison, is different gods better
or is Allāh, the One, the Dominant.**

Sayyidunā Yūsuf ﷺ is reasoning with the two youngsters. Rather
than having multiple gods-one for each task– isn't it better to have
Allāh ﷻ the One, Who overpowers everything else?

$$مَا تَعْبُدُونَ مِنْ دُونِهِ إِلَّا أَسْمَاءً سَمَّيْتُمُوهَا أَنْتُمْ وَآبَاؤُكُمْ مَا أَنْزَلَ اللهُ بِهَا مِنْ سُلْطَانٍ إِنِ الْحُكْمُ إِلَّا لِلّهِ أَمَرَ أَلَّا تَعْبُدُوا إِلَّا إِيَّاهُ ذَلِكَ الدِّينُ الْقَيِّمُ وَلَكِنَّ أَكْثَرَ النَّاسِ لَا يَعْلَمُونَ$$

**[40] You don't worship other than Allāh but names which you
and your fathers have kept. Allāh has not revealed any evidence
regarding it. There is no judgement except Allāh's. He has com-**

manded that you worship no one except Him. That is the correct religion, but most of the people do not know.

Sayyidunā Yūsuf عليه السلام has given the nasīhat (advice) and now as promised, he tells them about their dreams.

$$يَا صَاحِبَيِ السِّجْنِ أَمَّا أَحَدُكُمَا فَيَسْقِيْ رَبَّهٗ خَمْرًا ۚ وَأَمَّا الْآخَرُ فَيُصْلَبُ فَتَأْكُلُ الطَّيْرُ مِنْ رَّأْسِهٖ ۚ قُضِيَ الْأَمْرُ الَّذِيْ فِيْهِ تَسْتَفْتِيَانِ$$

[41] O the two companions of the prison, regarding one of you, he will give drink to his lord. And regarding the other, he will be crucified and the birds will eat from his head. The matter has already been destined regarding which both of you asked.

Sayyidunā Yūsuf عليه السلام related the interpretation of their dreams at this stage. The first one, who saw himself making wine, will feed his leader. The word 'Rabb' in the Egyptian language means 'leader' so this is not referring to Allāh ﷻ, rather Egypt's leader. The second one will be crucified.

$$وَقَالَ لِلَّذِيْ ظَنَّ أَنَّهٗ نَاجٍ مِّنْهُمَا اذْكُرْنِيْ عِنْدَ رَبِّكَ فَأَنْسَاهُ الشَّيْطَانُ ذِكْرَ رَبِّهٖ فَلَبِثَ فِي السِّجْنِ بِضْعَ سِنِيْنَ$$

[42] And he said to the person who he thought would be getting the salvation, "Remember me in the presence of your leader."

But Shaytān made him forget. So he remained in the prison for several years.

These two youngsters were involved in an act of treason. They tried to kill the king. It was found that one of them was guilty and the other would be reinstated as the palace cook. Hence, Sayyidunā Yūsuf الَعليه asked the one who would be reinstated for a simple task, to mention him in front of the king. However, he did not do this and as a result, Sayyidunā Yūsuf الَعليه remained in the prison for more years.

The King's Dream

وَقَالَ الْمَلِكُ إِنِّيْ أَرٰى سَبْعَ بَقَرَاتٍ سِمَانٍ يَّأْكُلُهُنَّ سَبْعٌ عِجَافٌ وَّسَبْعَ سُنْبُلَاتٍ خُضْرٍ وَّأُخَرَ يَابِسَاتٍ ۖ يَاۤأَيُّهَا الْمَلَاُ أَفْتُوْنِيْ فِيْ رُءْيَايَ إِنْ كُنْتُمْ لِلرُّءْيَا تَعْبُرُوْنَ

[43] And the king said, "Indeed I saw seven fat cows, seven weak cows were eating them and seven green ears of corn and others which were dried. O the ministers, give me the answer regarding my dream if you have knowledge regarding the dreams."

The king of Egypt at the time saw a very strange dream. He saw seven fat cows being eaten by seven weaker cows. Then he saw seven healthy ears of corn being overtaken by dry ones. As he was confused about this dream, he consulted the ministers of Egypt.

قَالُوْۤا أَضْغَاثُ أَحْلَامٍ ۖ وَمَا نَحْنُ بِتَأْوِيْلِ الْأَحْلَامِ بِعَالِمِيْنَ

[44] They said, "These are confused dreams. And regarding dreams we are not knowledgeable."

The ministers told the king that his dream was very strange and even if it wasn't, they do not possess the knowledge regarding dreams.

وَقَالَ الَّذِي نَجَا مِنْهُمَا وَادَّكَرَ بَعْدَ أُمَّةٍ أَنَا أُنَبِّئُكُمْ بِتَأْوِيلِهِ فَأَرْسِلُونِ

[45] And the one who was saved from the two and remembered after a long time said, "I will inform you regarding it's meaning, so send me."

The youngster who saw himself making wine in his dream and was freed from prison, finally remembered Sayyidunā Yūsuf ﷺ. He asked the king for permission to see Sayyidunā Yūsuf ﷺ in prison, to which he agreed.

يُوسُفُ أَيُّهَا الصِّدِّيقُ أَفْتِنَا فِي سَبْعِ بَقَرَاتٍ سِمَانٍ يَأْكُلُهُنَّ سَبْعٌ عِجَافٌ وَسَبْعِ سُنْبُلَاتٍ خُضْرٍ وَأُخَرَ يَابِسَاتٍ لَّعَلِّي أَرْجِعُ إِلَى النَّاسِ لَعَلَّهُمْ يَعْلَمُونَ

[46] "Yūsuf! O the truthful one, give us the answer regarding the seven fat cows which the seven thin cows were eating and the seven green ears of corn and the others which were very dry. So I could return back towards the people so that they know."

Allāh ﷻ informs us in this verse how the youngster came back to Sayyidunā Yūsuf ﷺ for another favour. Subhān-Allāh! the quality of the pious people was such, that they would overlook the people's mistakes. This person that came to Sayyidunā Yūsuf ﷺ was so selfish. After he was told of his dream, he did not care to uphold what he was asked. He did not remember Sayyidunā Yūsuf ﷺ prior to this. And again, only remembered him because the need arose.

Despite this, he *still* came to Sayyidunā Yūsuf ﷺ because he realised, although he is selfish, Sayyidunā Yūsuf ﷺ is self-less. This was the quality of our pious predecessors. Sayyidunā Yūsuf ﷺ did not scold him, he didn't even remind him of it.

قَالَ تَزْرَعُوْنَ سَبْعَ سِنِيْنَ دَأَبًا فَمَا حَصَدْتُّمْ فَذَرُوْهُ فِيْ سُنْبُلِهٖ إِلَّا قَلِيْلًا مِّمَّا تَأْكُلُوْنَ

[47] He said, "You will grow crops for seven years continuously, whatever you harvest, leave them in the ears but a small amount from which you will eat.

Sayyidunā Yūsuf ﷺ immediately answered the request. He explained that the seven fat cows and green ears of corn refer to seven prosperous years of harvest. Whilst the seven thin, weak cows and dry ears of corn symbolize the seven years of famine which are to come after the good harvest. Finally, Sayyidunā Yūsuf ﷺ told him the solution for the problem.

ثُمَّ يَأْتِي مِنْ بَعْدِ ذَلِكَ سَبْعٌ شِدَادٌ يَأْكُلْنَ مَا قَدَّمْتُمْ لَهُنَّ إِلَّا قَلِيلًا مِّمَّا تُحْصِنُونَ ثُمَّ يَأْتِي مِنْ بَعْدِ ذَلِكَ عَامٌ فِيهِ يُغَاثُ النَّاسُ وَفِيهِ يَعْصِرُونَ

[48] "Thereafter seven difficult years will follow that you will consume all that you would have stored for them except the little that you leave. [49] Then will come after that a year in which the people will be given rain and in which they will press [olives and grapes]."

Sayyidunā Yūsuf ﷺ explains that the seven years of good harvest will be followed by seven years of drought and famine. Then, on the fifteenth year, the people will be in a good state because of the rain and in that they will be squeezing the juice. The people will be utilising the vastness of the crops by obtaining different juices from them.

وَقَالَ الْمَلِكُ ائْتُونِي بِهِ ۖ فَلَمَّا جَاءَهُ الرَّسُولُ قَالَ ارْجِعْ إِلَى رَبِّكَ فَاسْأَلْهُ مَا بَالُ النِّسْوَةِ اللَّاتِي قَطَّعْنَ أَيْدِيَهُنَّ ۚ إِنَّ رَبِّي بِكَيْدِهِنَّ عَلِيمٌ

[50] The king said, "Bring him to me." So when the messenger came to him, he said, "Return to your lord and ask him what is the situation of those women who cut their fingers. Indeed my Lord knows regarding their conspiracy."

When the king was informed about Sayyidunā Yūsuf's ﷺ dream interpretation, he was so astounded and impressed. He immediately told his ministers to summon Sayyidunā Yūsuf ﷺ. 'Messenger' here does not mean a prophet, it means the ambassador.

Sayyidunā Yūsuf's ﷺ Innocence is Revealed

We must remember that Sayyidunā Yūsuf ﷺ was wrongfully imprisoned. He was never guilty of the crime he was incited towards. Hence, if he was to emerge from the prison, people would see him and talk about the allegations that were attributed to him. Because of this, he wanted to clarify the situation and make his innocence apparent. This is a very important lesson that we must inculcate in our lives. If we know that somebody is being wronged we should seek to clarify the misconception.

Furthermore, Sayyidunā Yūsuf ﷺ did not shame Zulaikha, he mentioned the incident of the women cutting their hands because this was popular amongst the people.

After hearing this, the king summoned the womenfolk and put them to trial.

قَالَ مَا خَطْبُكُنَّ إِذْ رَاوَدْتُّنَّ يُوْسُفَ عَنْ نَّفْسِهِ ۚ قُلْنَ حَاشَ لِلّٰهِ مَا عَلِمْنَا عَلَيْهِ مِنْ سُوْءٍ ۚ قَالَتِ امْرَأَتُ الْعَزِيْزِ الْآنَ حَصْحَصَ الْحَقُّ أَنَا رَاوَدْتُّهُ عَنْ نَّفْسِهِ وَإِنَّهُ لَمِنَ الصَّادِقِيْنَ

[51] He said, "What is your situation when you all incited Yūsuf against him?" They said, "Allāh forbid. We don't know anything wrong regarding him." The wife of Azīz Misr said, "Now the truth has come out. I was the one that seduced him against his Nafs and indeed he was of the truthful."

The women confessed the truth regarding Sayyidunā Yūsuf ﷺ. Zulaikha finally admitted she was in the wrong and Sayyidunā Yūsuf ﷺ was innocent.

ذَٰلِكَ لِيَعْلَمَ أَنِّي لَمْ أَخُنْهُ بِالْغَيْبِ وَأَنَّ اللَّهَ لَا يَهْدِي كَيْدَ الْخَائِنِينَ

[52] "That is so that the Azīz will know I did not betray him in (his) absence and that Allāh does not guide the plan of betrayers.

Sayyidunā Yūsuf ﷺ wanted to clarify his innocence, especially to Azīz Misr. He proved his purity and chastity from the testimonies of the guilty parties. Subhān-Allāh, being the humble man he was, he didn't want to paint himself as so pure, so he said…

وَمَا أُبَرِّئُ نَفْسِي ۚ إِنَّ النَّفْسَ لَأَمَّارَةٌ بِالسُّوءِ إِلَّا مَا رَحِمَ رَبِّي ۚ إِنَّ رَبِّي غَفُورٌ رَّحِيمٌ

[53] And I do not claim myself that I am pure. Indeed the Nafs always orders to something bad except those upon which

my Lord has mercy. Indeed, my Lord is Forgiving and Merciful."

Sayyidunā Yūsuf ﷺ Becomes Egypt's Treasurer

وَقَالَ الْمَلِكُ ائْتُوْنِيْ بِهِ أَسْتَخْلِصْهُ لِنَفْسِيْ ۖ فَلَمَّا كَلَّمَهُ قَالَ إِنَّكَ الْيَوْمَ لَدَيْنَا مَكِيْنٌ أَمِيْنٌ

[54] And the king said, "Bring him to me, I will make him sincerely for myself." Then when he spoke to him, he said, "Indeed today you are in a respectable position within our presence"

The king held Sayyidunā Yūsuf ﷺ in high rank and respect. This was such, that he appointed him as the person in charge of all the financial dealings within Egypt. He became the treasurer of Egypt. In essence, he was running Egypt just without the title. By name he was the finance minister but in reality he was the practical king who would carry out all the work.

قَالَ اجْعَلْنِيْ عَلَى خَزَائِنِ الْأَرْضِ ۖ إِنِّيْ حَفِيْظٌ عَلِيْمٌ

[55] He (Yūsuf) said, "Appoint me upon the treasures of the earth. Indeed I am the one who preserves and is the most knowledgeable."

Sayyidunā Yūsuf الَّلا asked to be the finance minister of Egypt because he possessed the two qualities that such a role requires; trust
and knowledge. Both qualities are needed to successfully look after
Egypt's treasury. If a person was knowledgeable enough to know
how to deal with the finances, but had a deceiving character, this
would be a problem. A fraudulent and cheating individual who takes
over a country's finances is the recipe for disaster. Similarly, if a person is trustworthy, but does not possess the knowledge of how and
when to spend the money, then this is equally destructive. Hoarding
money when it needs to be spent is just as bad as spending money
foolishly. Hence, both qualities complement each other and are
equally needed.

$$وَكَذَٰلِكَ مَكَّنَّا لِيُوسُفَ فِي الْأَرْضِ يَتَبَوَّأُ مِنْهَا حَيْثُ يَشَاءُ ۚ نُصِيبُ بِرَحْمَتِنَا مَن نَّشَاءُ ۖ وَلَا نُضِيعُ أَجْرَ الْمُحْسِنِينَ$$

[56] **And in this way We gave authority to Yūsuf on the earth.
He used to live wherever he wished. We give with Our mercy to whoever We wish. And We do not destroy the reward
of those people who carry out good deeds.**

Allāh ﷻ makes reference to His sublime mercy which He bestowed
upon Sayyidunā Yūsuf الَّلا. Out of His infinite mercy, Allāh ﷻ took
Sayyidunā Yūsuf الَّلا out of the well and gave him dignity, respect
and honour.

Again, Allāh ﷻ reminds us that our reward is never lost. Every good deed that you do, you will *always* be rewarded for it. Effort and striving for sake of Allāh ﷻ can never go wasted.

وَلَأَجْرُ الْآخِرَةِ خَيْرٌ لِّلَّذِينَ آمَنُوا وَكَانُوا يَتَّقُونَ

[57] And the reward of the Hereafter is better for those who believe and fear Allāh.

In this verse, Allāh ﷻ gives us hope and motivation. Allāh ﷻ blessed Sayyidunā Yūsuf ﷺ massively in this world, but this doesn't compare to the Hereafter. One cannot comprehend the blessings in Jannah, which are far superior to anything of this world. Everybody will be receiving reward in this world but in the Hereafter, the pious people and the Muslims will get unimaginable reward.

The next verse continues with the story.

وَجَاءَ إِخْوَةُ يُوسُفَ فَدَخَلُوا عَلَيْهِ فَعَرَفَهُمْ وَهُمْ لَهُ مُنكِرُونَ

[58] And the brothers of Yūsuf came and they entered upon Yūsuf. He recognised them and they did not recognise him.

As we know, Sayyidunā Yūsuf's ﷺ dream interpretation came true, and the seven years of famine were taking their toll amongst the land. Even Kan'ān, where Sayyidunā Yūsuf ﷺ was from, had been affected by the harsh famine. The brothers of Sayyidunā Yūsuf ﷺ

had heard about a generous ruler in Egypt that would give food to people. Because of this, the ten brothers set out for Egypt, in pursuit of food. They had no idea that this generous ruler was their long lost brother.

Exactly how the verse explains, the brothers entered upon Sayyidunā Yūsuf ﷺ, who instantly recognized them. The last time they would have seen each other, Sayyidunā Yūsuf was young but the brothers were older. When a person get's older, their facial expressions remain apparent, which is why Sayyidunā Yūsuf ﷺ was able to recognise them. But Sayyidunā Yūsuf was a young boy the last time they had seen him, so they had no idea it was him, because he had grown so much.

Whilst they were mentioning their need to Sayyidunā Yūsuf ﷺ, he would ask them questions. He asked them "Who is your father?" and they replied "Our father is a Prophet." He said, "How many brothers are you?" to which the brothers said, "We are twelve, one of our brothers was eaten by a wolf." Subhān-Allāh. They were saying this to Sayyidunā Yūsuf ﷺ.

وَلَمَّا جَهَّزَهُم بِجَهَازِهِمْ قَالَ ائْتُونِي بِأَخٍ لَّكُم مِّنْ أَبِيكُمْ ۚ أَلَا تَرَوْنَ أَنِّي أُوفِي الْكَيْلَ وَأَنَا خَيْرُ الْمُنزِلِينَ

[59] And when he prepared for them their preparation , he said, "Bring to me your brother from your father. Don't you see

that I am giving you full. And I am the best of all people who show hospitality."

When Sayyidunā Yūsuf ﷺ asked about the other brother who was left behind (Binyāmīn), they said, "Our father is fearful about Binyāmīn because of what happened to our other brother." So, Sayyidunā Yūsuf ﷺ told them to bring Binyāmīn, otherwise they wouldn't get any food next time. Subhān-Allāh! out of his kindness, he gave the brothers their share plus Binyāmīn's, despite him not coming with them.

Sayyidunā Yūsuf ﷺ mentions that he is the best of hosts, which was true. Sayyidunā Yūsuf ﷺ looked after them very well. When they arrived, he placed them in the big guest room, which is usually meant for very important people. He ordered his workers to respect and feed them well.

فَإِن لَّمْ تَأْتُونِي بِهِ فَلَا كَيْلَ لَكُمْ عِندِي وَلَا تَقْرَبُونِ

[60] But if you do not bring him to me, no measure will there be for you from me, nor will you approach me."

Sayyidunā Yūsuf ﷺ threatens them of no loads if they come to Egypt without Binyāmīn.

قَالُوا سَنُرَاوِدُ عَنْهُ أَبَاهُ وَإِنَّا لَفَاعِلُونَ

[61] They said, "We will attempt to dissuade his father from (keeping) him, and indeed we will do (it)."

Sayyidunā Yūsuf's الﷺ Generosity

وَقَالَ لِفِتْيَانِهِ اجْعَلُوا بِضَاعَتَهُمْ فِي رِحَالِهِمْ لَعَلَّهُمْ يَعْرِفُوْنَهَا إِذَا انقَلَبُوا إِلَى أَهْلِهِمْ لَعَلَّهُمْ يَرْجِعُوْنَ

[62] And (Yūsuf) said to his servants, "Put their merchandise into their saddlebags so they might recognize it when they have gone back to their people that perhaps they will (again) return."

Sayyidunā Yūsuf الﷺ put the money that they used to pay for their loads back into his brother's luggage. Subhān-Allāh! Despite the brother's evilness towards him and denying the truth, he couldn't accept money from his own brothers.

فَلَمَّا رَجَعُوا إِلَى أَبِيهِمْ قَالُوا يَا أَبَانَا مُنِعَ مِنَّا الْكَيْلُ فَأَرْسِلْ مَعَنَا أَخَانَا نَكْتَلْ وَإِنَّا لَهُ لَحَافِظُوْنَ

[63] So when they returned to their father, they said, "O our father, (further) measure has been denied to us, so send with us our brother (that) we will be given measure. And indeed we will be his guardians."

When they reached the stage where the food Sayyidunā Yūsuf ﷺ provided was running out, they started to make plans of returning to Egypt. Of course, they remembered Sayyidunā Yūsuf's ﷺ condition of the future food and began to ask their father to allow Binyāmīn to join them.

قَالَ هَلْ آمَنُكُمْ عَلَيْهِ إِلَّا كَمَا أَمِنْتُكُمْ عَلَى أَخِيهِ مِنْ قَبْلُ ۖ فَاللّٰهُ خَيْرٌ حَافِظًا ۖ وَهُوَ أَرْحَمُ الرَّاحِمِينَ

[64] He said, "Should I entrust you with him except (under coercion) as I entrusted you with his brother before? But Allāh is the Best Guardian, and He is the Most Merciful of the merciful."

Sayyidunā Ya'qūb ﷺ was hesitant. The first time he entrusted them with Sayyidunā Yūsuf ﷺ, he never saw him again. And now they were asking for Binyāmīn, the only one left who he held so dearly in his company. But this was Allāh's ﷻ plan. And Allāh ﷻ was testing Sayyidunā Ya'qūb ﷺ also.

وَلَمَّا فَتَحُوا مَتَاعَهُمْ وَجَدُوا بِضَاعَتَهُمْ رُدَّتْ إِلَيْهِمْ ۖ قَالُوا يَا أَبَانَا مَا نَبْغِي ۖ هٰذِهِ بِضَاعَتُنَا رُدَّتْ إِلَيْنَا ۖ وَنَمِيرُ أَهْلَنَا وَنَحْفَظُ أَخَانَا وَنَزْدَادُ كَيْلَ بَعِيرٍ ۖ ذٰلِكَ كَيْلٌ يَّسِيرٌ

[65] And when they opened their baggage, they found their merchandise returned to them. They said, "O our father, what (more) could we desire? This is our merchandise returned to us.

And we will obtain supplies for our family and protect our brother and obtain an increase of a camel's load; that is an easy measurement."

When the brothers opened their goods, they were surprised to find their payment inside. This only reinforced them to go again. They realised that with Binyāmīn, they could obtain at least one camel load more for the family. All they had to do was bring him along. Hence, they continued to convince Sayyidunā Ya'qūb عليه السلام to allow Binyāmīn to join them.

قَالَ لَنْ أُرْسِلَهُ مَعَكُمْ حَتّٰى تُؤْتُوْنِ مَوْثِقًا مِّنَ اللّٰهِ لَتَأْتُنَّنِيْ بِهِ إِلَّا أَنْ يُّحَاطَ بِكُمْ ۚ فَلَمَّا آتَوْهُ مَوْثِقَهُمْ قَالَ اللّٰهُ عَلٰى مَا نَقُوْلُ وَكِيْلٌ

[66] Ya'qūb said, "Never will I send him with you until you give me a promise by Allāh that you will bring him (back) to me, unless you should be surrounded." And when they had given their promise, he said, " Allāh, over what we say is Witness."

Sayyidunā Ya'qūb عليه السلام made them swear by Allāh عزّوجلّ that they would bring Binyāmīn back, unless something happens outside their control. Hence they made the promise.

The Evil Eye

وَقَالَ يَا بَنِيَّ لَا تَدْخُلُوا مِنْ بَابٍ وَاحِدٍ وَّادْخُلُوا مِنْ أَبْوَابٍ مُّتَفَرِّقَةٍ ۖ وَمَا أُغْنِي عَنكُم مِّنَ اللّهِ مِن شَيْءٍ ۖ إِنِ الْحُكْمُ إِلَّا لِلّهِ ۖ عَلَيْهِ تَوَكَّلْتُ ۖ وَعَلَيْهِ فَلْيَتَوَكَّلِ الْمُتَوَكِّلُونَ

[67]And he said, "O my sons, do not enter from one gate but enter from different gates; and I cannot avail you against (the decree of) Allāh at all. The decision is only for Allāh; upon Him I have relied, and upon Him let those who would rely (indeed) rely."

Sayyidunā Ya'qūb ﷺ gave his sons important advice. He advised them to enter through different gates when entering Egypt, lest they are afflicted with an evil eye. Sayyidunā Ya'qūb ﷺ recognized that his sons were a big, strong, handsome group of men, who would be ideal prey to Nazr (evil eye). Hence, he came up with a solution.

Indeed, the evil eye is true. As a matter of fact, one of the worst killers is Nazr. We must always protect ourselves and others from this mass murderer by taking the correct precautions. One is by reciting:

مَا شَاءَ اللّهُ لَا قُوَّةَ إِلَّا بِاللّهِ

Whatever Allāh has willed. There is no power except with Allāh. (18:39)

Despite taking the precautionary measures to protect oneself from Nazr, if one is still afflicted then this is the Qadr of Allāh ﷻ (decree). We need to understand that yes-we take the measures- but whatever happens after that is the divine decree of Allāh ﷻ. For further details on this topic you can study my teacher's book - Sleepers of the Cave - under the 39th verse.

وَلَمَّا دَخَلُوْا مِنْ حَيْثُ أَمَرَهُمْ أَبُوْهُمْ مَّاكَانَ يُغْنِي عَنْهُمْ مِّنَ اللّٰهِ مِنْ شَيْءٍ إِلَّا حَاجَةً فِيْ نَفْسِ يَعْقُوْبَ قَضَاهَاؕ وَإِنَّهُ لَذُوْ عِلْمٍ لِّمَا عَلَّمْنَاهُ وَلٰكِنَّ أَكْثَرَ النَّاسِ لَا يَعْلَمُوْنَ

[68]And when they entered from where their father had ordered them, it did not avail them against Allāh at all except (it was) a need within the soul of Ya'qūb, which he satisfied. And indeed, he was a possessor of knowledge because of what We had taught him, but most of the people do not know.

وَلَمَّا دَخَلُوْا عَلٰى يُوْسُفَ آوٰى إِلَيْهِ أَخَاهُۖ قَالَ إِنِّيْ أَنَا أَخُوْكَ فَلَا تَبْتَئِسْ بِمَا كَانُوْا يَعْمَلُوْنَ

[69]And when they entered upon Yūsuf, he took his brother to himself; he said, "Indeed I am your brother, so do not despair over what they used to do (to me)."

Subhān-Allāh! When the brothers arrived with Binyāmīn, Sayyidunā Yūsuf ﷺ instantly took him to the side and told him that he was his brother, Yūsuf!

Allāh's ﷻ Plan for Binyāmīn

فَلَمَّا جَهَّزَهُم بِجَهَازِهِمْ جَعَلَ السِّقَايَةَ فِي رَحْلِ أَخِيهِ ثُمَّ أَذَّنَ مُؤَذِّنٌ أَيَّتُهَا الْعِيرُ إِنَّكُمْ لَسَارِقُونَ

[70] So when he had furnished them with their supplies, he put the (gold measuring) bowl into the bag of his brother. Then an announcer called out, "O caravan, indeed you are thieves."

Sayyidunā Yūsuf عليه السلام wanted to keep his beloved brother Binyāmīn with him, so he prayed to Allāh ﷻ. Allāh ﷻ made a divine plan enabling Binyāmīn to stay with Sayyidunā Yūsuf عليه السلام in Egypt. There was a gold bowl that they would use in the palace for measuring items. Of course, as the brothers had the best hospitality when they would come to Egypt, staying in the noble palace, it made sense if they had stolen it whilst they were there. So, this was the perfect accusation to place on the brothers. Sayyidunā Yūsuf عليه السلام placed the gold measuring bowl into Binyāmīn's belongings. Shortly after, the brothers were summoned and asked about the bowl.

قَالُوا وَأَقْبَلُوا عَلَيْهِم مَّاذَا تَفْقِدُونَ

[71] They said while approaching them, "What is it you are missing?"

قَالُوا نَفْقِدُ صُوَاعَ الْمَلِكِ وَلِمَن جَاءَ بِهِ حِمْلُ بَعِيرٍ وَأَنَا بِهِ زَعِيمٌ

[72] They said, "We are missing the measure of the king. And for he who produces it, is (the reward of) a camel's load, and I am responsible for it."

قَالُوا تَاللَّهِ لَقَدْ عَلِمْتُم مَّا جِئْنَا لِنُفْسِدَ فِي الْأَرْضِ وَمَا كُنَّا سَارِقِينَ

[73] They said, "By Allāh, you have certainly known that we did not come to cause corruption in the land, and we are not thieves."

Acknowledging the accusation, the brothers assured them of their innocence from this crime.

قَالُوا فَمَا جَزَاؤُهُ إِن كُنتُمْ كَاذِبِينَ

[74] The accusers said, "Then what would be its recompense if you should be liars?"

قَالُوا جَزَاؤُهُ مَن وُجِدَ فِي رَحْلِهِ فَهُوَ جَزَاؤُهُ كَذَلِكَ نَجْزِي الظَّالِمِينَ

[75] (The brothers) said, "Its recompense is that he in whose bag it is found - he (himself) will be its recompense. Thus do we recompense the wrongdoers."

In the Sharīah of Sayyidunā Yūsuf عليه السلام and Sayyidunā Ya'qūb عليه السلام, if a person stole from somebody, then the thief would become the slave of that person whom he had stolen from. Sayyidunā Yūsuf عليه السلام knew this, which is why he placed the gold bowl in Binyāmīn's luggage so he would *have* to stay with him. There was no other way to keep a person belonging to a different country besides this. Allāh ﷻ made the brothers say the recompense themselves, so they could only blame themselves for what was to occur.

فَبَدَأَ بِأَوْعِيَتِهِمْ قَبْلَ وِعَاءِ أَخِيهِ ثُمَّ اسْتَخْرَجَهَا مِنْ وِعَاءِ أَخِيهِ ۚ كَذَٰلِكَ كِدْنَا لِيُوسُفَ ۖ مَا كَانَ لِيَأْخُذَ أَخَاهُ فِي دِينِ الْمَلِكِ إِلَّا أَن يَّشَاءَ اللَّهُ ۚ نَرْفَعُ دَرَجَاتٍ مَّن نَّشَاءُ ۗ وَفَوْقَ كُلِّ ذِي عِلْمٍ عَلِيمٌ

[76] So he began (the search) with their bags before the bag of his brother; then he extracted it from the bag of his brother. Thus did We plan for Yūsuf. He could not have taken his brother within the religion of the king except that Allāh willed. We raise in degrees whom We will, but over every possessor of knowledge is one (more) knowing.

They knew which bag they hid the gold bowl in, so cleverly, they started with the other brothers' bags and came to the actual one later to avoid even an iota amount of suspicion. Subhān-Allāh! Look at the plan of Allāh ﷻ. Totally free from any fault, amazing and sublime!

قَالُوٓا إِن يَسْرِقْ فَقَدْ سَرَقَ أَخٌ لَّهُ مِن قَبْلُ ۚ فَأَسَرَّهَا يُوسُفُ فِى نَفْسِهِ وَلَمْ يُبْدِهَا لَهُمْ ۚ قَالَ أَنتُمْ شَرٌّ مَّكَانًا ۖ وَاللّٰهُ أَعْلَمُ بِمَا تَصِفُونَ

**[77] They said, "If he steals - a brother of his has stolen before."
But Yūsuf kept it within himself and did not reveal it to
them. He said, "You are worse in position, and Allāh is
most knowing of what you describe. "**

When Sayyidunā Yūsuf ﷺ was very young, he went to his Khāla's
(maternal aunt) house. She didn't want to return Sayyidunā Yūsuf
ﷺ so she put goods in his bag in order to keep him with her according to the Sharīah of Ya'qūb ﷺ. This is the event being referred to in
this verse.

قَالُوا يَا أَيُّهَا الْعَزِيزُ إِنَّ لَهُ أَبًا شَيْخًا كَبِيرًا فَخُذْ أَحَدَنَا مَكَانَهُ ۖ إِنَّا نَرَاكَ مِنَ الْمُحْسِنِينَ

**[78] They said, "O 'Azīz, indeed he has a father (who is) an old
man, so take one of us in place of him. Indeed, we see you
as a doer of good."**

At this point, they started to plead with Sayyidunā Yūsuf ﷺ."Please
take someone else, we made a promise to our father, we can't leave
him behind."

قَالَ مَعَاذَ اللّٰهِ أَن نَّأْخُذَ إِلَّا مَن وَّجَدْنَا مَتَاعَنَا عِندَهُ إِنَّا إِذًا لَّظَالِمُونَ

[79] He said, "(I seek) the refuge of Allāh (to prevent) that we take except him with whom we found our possession. Indeed we would then be unjust."

Sayyidunā Yūsuf السلام of course, played along to the plan. He said, مَعَاذَ اللّٰهِ —"How can we take someone else in his place. *He* is the criminal. So all the brothers remained completely despaired and lost all hope.

فَلَمَّا اسْتَيْأَسُوا مِنْهُ خَلَصُوا نَجِيًّا ۖ قَالَ كَبِيرُهُمْ أَلَمْ تَعْلَمُوا أَنَّ أَبَاكُمْ قَدْ أَخَذَ عَلَيْكُم مَّوْثِقًا مِّنَ اللّٰهِ وَمِن قَبْلُ مَا فَرَّطتُمْ فِي يُوسُفَ ۖ فَلَنْ أَبْرَحَ الْأَرْضَ حَتَّى يَأْذَنَ لِي أَبِي أَوْ يَحْكُمَ اللّٰهُ لِي ۖ وَهُوَ خَيْرُ الْحَاكِمِينَ

[80] So when they all became despaired from him, they went to one side for whispers. The eldest one said, "Don't you know that your father has taken from you a promise from Allāh and prior to this, what you have caused (problems) regarding Yūsuf. So I will not move from the earth until my father gives me permission or Allāh judges regarding me, and He is the best of all judges."

كَبِيرُهُمْ has two meanings:

1. The most senior in terms of intelligence.
2. The most senior in terms of age.

There are two conditions:

If my father hears about this matter and he says it is fine and I am happy with you then I will return back.

If Allāh ﷻ miraculously intervenes e.g that our brother is allowed to come back with us, then I will return back.

In the following verse, the eldest says to the other brothers,

ارْجِعُوٓا إِلَىٰٓ أَبِيكُمْ فَقُولُوا يَٰٓأَبَانَآ إِنَّ ابْنَكَ سَرَقَ وَمَا شَهِدْنَآ إِلَّا بِمَا عَلِمْنَا وَمَا كُنَّا لِلْغَيْبِ حَافِظِينَ

[81] "Return back to your father and say, "O our father indeed your son has stolen." And we are not witness but of the things we know and we are not the protectors of the unseen."

The eldest brother tells the brothers to tell the situation to their father and let him decide for himself. They refer to Binyāmīn as "your son" not "our brother" as he was the step-brother; not the real biological brother. We just saw the cup come out from his luggage and if something happened in our absence, we cannot preserve that, only Allāh ﷻ knows. To make this a concrete and strong point to the father, they said,

وَاسْأَلِ الْقَرْيَةَ الَّتِي كُنَّا فِيهَا وَالْعِيرَ الَّتِي أَقْبَلْنَا فِيهَا وَإِنَّا لَصَادِقُونَ

[82]"And ask the (people of the) village in which we also from and that caravan that we have come. Indeed we are truthful."

There are two evidences the brothers are putting forth to show they are truthful.

1. Look and ask the people of the village.
2. Look at the caravan that came in.

The brothers did not lie to the father this time. However, because they lied once before, the father did not believe them. Once a person lies, he will always be considered a liar.

قَالَ بَلْ سَوَّلَتْ لَكُمْ أَنفُسُكُمْ أَمْرًا فَصَبْرٌ جَمِيلٌ عَسَى اللّٰهُ أَن يَأْتِيَنِي بِهِمْ جَمِيعًا إِنَّهُ هُوَ الْعَلِيمُ الْحَكِيمُ

**[83]" Yaʿqūb said, "Your soul has beautified the matter for you."
So patience is good. It is hoped from Allāh, that He will bring all
my (three) sons back to me. Indeed, He is the One Who is the
Most Knowledgeable, the Most Wise."**

There are three types of Sabr (patience):

1. صَبْرٌ فِي الْمُصِيْبَةِ - Patience at the time of difficulty.

2. صَبْرٌ عَلَى الْإِطَاعَةِ - Patience upon carrying out the obedience of Allāh سبحانه وتعالى.

3. صَبْرٌ عَنِ الْمَعْصِيَةِ - Patience from staying away from sins.

Sayyidunā Ya'qūb عليه السلام Becomes Blind

وَتَوَلَّىٰ عَنْهُمْ وَقَالَ يَاۤ اَسَفٰى عَلٰى يُوْسُفَ وَابْيَضَّتْ عَيْنَاهُ مِنَ الْحُزْنِ فَهُوَ كَظِيْمٌ

[84] And he turned away from them and said, "O my sorrow over Yūsuf ," and his eyes became white from grief, for he was (of that) a suppressor.

Sayyidunā Ya'qūb عليه السلام became so upset, distraught and grieved that he cried until his blessed eyes became dry. His eyes became completely white, resulting in blindness.

Sayyidunā Ya'qūb عليه السلام practised beautiful patience. Many people have a distorted understanding of Sabr. They think that for a person to have patience, they must be firm, hold in their tears and become emotionless when dealing with affliction. However, this is completely false and even unhealthy. When a person is suffering grief, loss or death of a loved one, it is perfectly acceptable to be sad and cry, this is all part of the natural healing process. By suppressing these functional processes, it causes more harm to the person. In this verse, Allāh ﷻ informs us how Sayyidunā Ya'qūb ﷺ became blind out of crying for his beloved Yūsuf ﷺ. He was a strong Prophet of Allāh ﷻ, and Allāh ﷻ Himself describes his patience as beautiful. When our beloved Prophet Muhammad ﷺ lost his loved ones, he cried. Crying is not a sign of weakness, it is a perfectly natural aspect of our human nature.

قَالُوْا تَاللّٰهِ تَفْتَأُ تَذْكُرُ يُوْسُفَ حَتّٰى تَكُوْنَ حَرَضًا أَوْ تَكُوْنَ مِنَ الْهَالِكِيْنَ

[85] They said, "By Allāh, you will not cease remembering Yūsuf until you become fatally ill or become of those who perish."

Still, they would say to Sayyidunā Ya'qūb ﷺ that he would become ill if he continued in this way.

قَالَ إِنَّمَا أَشْكُوْ بَثِّيْ وَحُزْنِيْ إِلَى اللّٰهِ وَأَعْلَمُ مِنَ اللّٰهِ مَا لَا تَعْلَمُوْنَ

[86] He said, "I only complain of my suffering and my grief to Allāh, and I know from Allāh that which you do not know.

Allāh ﷻ had informed Sayyidunā Ya'qūb ﷺ through revelation not to worry, he would see Sayyidunā Yūsuf ﷺ again.

يَا بَنِيَّ اذْهَبُوْا فَتَحَسَّسُوْا مِنْ يُّوْسُفَ وَأَخِيْهِ وَلَا تَيْأَسُوْا مِنْ رَّوْحِ اللّٰهِ ۖ إِنَّهٗ لَا يَيْأَسُ مِنْ رَّوْحِ اللّٰهِ إِلَّا الْقَوْمُ الْكَافِرُوْنَ

[87] O my sons, go and find out about Yūsuf and his brother and despair not of relief from Allāh. Indeed, no one despairs of relief from Allāh except the disbelieving people."

Believers should never ever lose hope in Allāh. Allāh ﷻ forgives all sins.

فَلَمَّا دَخَلُوْا عَلَيْهِ قَالُوْا يٰأَيُّهَا الْعَزِيْزُ مَسَّنَا وَأَهْلَنَا الضُّرُّ وَجِئْنَا بِبِضَاعَةٍ مُّزْجَاةٍ فَأَوْفِ لَنَا الْكَيْلَ وَتَصَدَّقْ عَلَيْنَا ۖ إِنَّ اللّٰهَ يَجْزِي الْمُتَصَدِّقِيْنَ

[88] So when they entered upon Yūsuf, they said, "O 'Azīz, adversity has touched us and our family, and we have come with goods poor in quality, but give us full measure and be charitable to us. Indeed, Allāh rewards the charitable."

The brothers returned to Sayyidunā Yūsuf ﷺ and explained their situation. The word الضُّرُّ refers to severe drought and extreme hunger. And so, Sayyidunā Yūsuf ﷺ became emotional looking at the situation of his family.

قَالَ هَلۡ عَلِمۡتُم مَّا فَعَلۡتُم بِيُوۡسُفَ وَأَخِيهِ إِذۡ أَنتُمۡ جَاهِلُوۡنَ

[89] He said, "Do you know what you did with Yūsuf and his brother when you were ignorant?"

In the previous verses we came across how Allāh ﷻ indicated that there would be a time where Sayyidunā Yūsuf عليه السلام would once remind his brothers of their oppression in the future. This is that time.

Brothers' Reunion

قَالُوۡا أَإِنَّكَ لَأَنتَ يُوۡسُفُ ۖ قَالَ أَنَا يُوۡسُفُ وَهٰذَا أَخِي ۖ قَدۡ مَنَّ اللهُ عَلَيۡنَا ۖ إِنَّهُ مَن يَتَّقِ وَيَصۡبِرۡ فَإِنَّ اللهَ لَا يُضِيعُ أَجۡرَ الۡمُحۡسِنِينَ

[90] They said, "Are you indeed Yūsuf?" He said "I am Yūsuf and this is my brother. Allāh has certainly favoured us. Indeed, he who fears Allāh and is patient, then indeed, Allāh does not allow to be lost the reward of those who do good."

Subhān-Allāh! finally the moment came when all twelve brothers were reunited again. After all those long and eventful years, all brothers becoming adults with families, Sayyidunā Yūsuf عليه السلام becoming the finance minister of Egypt and so on, the truth was made apparent.

قَالُوا تَاللَّهِ لَقَدْ آثَرَكَ اللَّهُ عَلَيْنَا وَإِن كُنَّا لَخَاطِئِينَ

[91] They said, "By Allāh, certainly Allāh preferred you over us, and indeed we have been sinners."

Now the brothers start to feel remorse over what they had done. They immediately accepted their mistake and regretted what they had done in the past.

قَالَ لَا تَثْرِيبَ عَلَيْكُمُ الْيَوْمَ ۖ يَغْفِرُ اللَّهُ لَكُمْ ۖ وَهُوَ أَرْحَمُ الرَّاحِمِينَ

[92] He said, "No blame will there be upon you today. Allāh will forgive you; and He is the Most Merciful of the merciful."

Allāhu-Akbar! Sayyidunā Yūsuf ﷺ makes no mention of how much trouble they put him in, or how could they dare throw him in the well. Nothing of the sort. He immediately accepted their apology and did not place blame on them.

Divine Miracle

اذْهَبُوا بِقَمِيصِي هَٰذَا فَأَلْقُوهُ عَلَىٰ وَجْهِ أَبِي يَأْتِ بَصِيرًا وَأْتُونِي بِأَهْلِكُمْ أَجْمَعِينَ

[93] Take this shirt of mine, and cast it over the face of my father; he will become seeing. And bring me your family, all together."

When the brothers returned back to their father and gave him Say-yidunā Yūsuf's ﷺ shirt, something miraculous happened. Allah ﷻ immediately returned Sayyidunā Ya'qūb's ﷺ sight back to him when he placed it over his face!

وَلَمَّا فَصَلَتِ الْعِيرُ قَالَ أَبُوهُمْ إِنِّي لَأَجِدُ رِيْحَ يُوسُفَ لَوْلَا أَنْ تُفَنِّدُوْنِ

[94] And when the caravan departed (from Egypt), their father said, "Indeed, I find the smell of Yūsuf (and would say that he was alive) if you did not think about me weakened in mind."

تُفَنِّدُوْنِ refers to senile or mentally disabled. It can be thought of as having dementia also. The brothers of Sayyidunā Yūsuf ﷺ thought their father (Sayyidunā Ya'qūb ﷺ) to be mentally weak and it had been many years since they had all seen Sayyidunā Yūsuf ﷺ, yet Sayyidunā Ya'qūb ﷺ is still adamant on finding Sayyidunā Yūsuf ﷺ. Allāh ﷻ wanted them all to reunite thus it was a miracle from Allāh ﷺ for Sayyidunā Ya'qūb ﷺ to smell the scent of Sayyidunā Yūsuf ﷺ from many miles away.

وَجَدَ literally means to find. However here it means 'I can feel the fragrance.'

قَالُوا تَاللَّهِ إِنَّكَ لَفِي ضَلَالِكَ الْقَدِيْمِ

[95] They said, "By Allāh, indeed you are in your (same) old error."

There are many ways one can take an oath in the Arabic language:

تَاللَّهِ by use of the letter ت

وَاللَّهِ by use of the letter و

بِاللَّهِ by use of the letter ب

لِلَّهِ by use of the letter ل

فَلَمَّا أَنْ جَاءَ الْبَشِيرُ أَلْقَاهُ عَلَى وَجْهِهِ فَارْتَدَّ بَصِيْرًا ۖ قَالَ أَلَمْ أَقُلْ لَّكُمْ إِنِّي أَعْلَمُ مِنَ اللَّهِ مَا لَا تَعْلَمُوْنَ

[96] "And when the bearer of good tidings arrived, he put it (the shirt) on his (Ya'qūb) face, and he turned into a sighted man. He (Ya'qūb) said, "Did I not tell you that I know from Allāh what you do not know?"

There are two ways this verse can be interpreted:

Allāh ﷻ miraculously restored the eyesight of Sayyidunā Ya'qūb ﷺ.

Sayyidunā Ya'qūb ﷺ had a deep attachment to his son, as a result, when the shirt of Sayyidunā Yūsuf ﷺ was placed in front of him, it was an ointment for him. The blessing of the shirt was such that when it touched Sayyidunā Ya'qūb ﷺ he was cured.

Brother's Guilt

Sayyidunā Ya'qūb ﷺ knew the brothers were not telling the truth when they plotted against Sayyidunā Yūsuf ﷺ and said to their father that Sayyidunā Yūsuf ﷺ had been eaten by a wolf. Thus he told the brothers that now he knows the truth. The brothers came and told their father,

قَالُوْا يَآ أَبَانَا اسْتَغْفِرْ لَنَا ذُنُوْبَنَا إِنَّا كُنَّا خَاطِئِيْنَ

[97] "They said, "Our father, pray to Allāh to forgive our sins. Surely, we have been guilty."

The word اِسْتَغْفِرْ means to ask for forgiveness. It is on the pattern of اِسْتِفْعَالٌ which gives the meaning of asking for something. For example, نَصَرَ means to help, اِسْتَنْصَرَ means to ask for help.

The root letters are غَفَرَ which means to forgive. The root letters of any word are very important. For example, the root letters ج ن. These letters give the meaning of something which is hidden.

جَنَّةٌ Paradise - These gardens are hidden from our eyes in this world.

جُنُوْنٌ Madness -This deficiency is hidden from the human eye.

جَنِيْنٌ Foetus -The unborn child is also hidden from our eyes.

جُنَّةٌ Shield -This hides a person from their enemies.

جِنْ -Jinn– A creation of Allāh ﷻ hidden from our eyes

$$قَالَ سَوْفَ أَسْتَغْفِرُ لَكُمْ رَبِّيْ إِنَّهُ هُوَ الْغَفُوْرُ الرَّحِيْمُ$$

[98] "He said, "Surely I will ask forgiveness for you from my Lord. Indeed, it is He Who is the Most-Forgiving, Most-Merciful."

Sayyidunā Ya'qūb ﷺ said, "I will surely ask forgiveness." The word he used was سَوْفَ which gives the meaning of something in the future. The question could arise as to why Sayyidunā Ya'qūb ﷺ asked for forgiveness later and not at that time. The scholars of Tafsīr mention Sayyidunā Ya'qūb ﷺ was waiting for the right moment which was at the time of Tahajjud as that time is a time in which Du'ās are accepted.

The Hadīth of the Holy Prophet ﷺ mentions, that Allāh ﷻ proclaims at the latter part of the night,

فَيَقُوْلُ هَلْ مِنْ مُسْتَغْفِرٍ فَأَغْفِرَ لَهُ هَلْ مِنْ سَائِلٍ فَأُعْطِيَهُ هَلْ مِنْ تَائِبٍ فَأَتُوْبَ عَلَيْهِ

"Allāh ﷻ says: Is there any one to ask for forgiveness so I may forgive him. Is there any one to ask (from Me) so I may give him (what he asks). Is there any one who is asking for forgiveness so I may forgive him?" (Dār Qutni)

Welcome to Egypt

فَلَمَّا دَخَلُوْا عَلٰى يُوْسُفَ اٰوٰى إِلَيْهِ أَبَوَيْهِ وَقَالَ ادْخُلُوْا مِصْرَ إِنْ شَاءَ اللهُ اٰمِنِيْنَ

[99] And when they entered upon Yūsuf, he placed his parents near himself and said, "Enter Egypt, Allāh willing in peace."

Sayyidunā Yūsuf عليه السلام instructed the person who took the shirt to Sayyidunā Ya'qūb عليه السلام to bring their whole family with them to Egypt so they can all reunite. Sayyidunā Yūsuf عليه السلام was the king of Egypt therefore for him to go to his father would prove difficult. The Holy Qur'ān is not telling the whole story as it is not a 'story book'. The main points which occurred are being mentioned in the Qur'ān.

أَبَوَيْهِ - This is referring to Sayyidunā Yūsuf's عليه السلام parents. As Sayyidunā Yūsuf's عليه السلام mother passed away, 'parents' refers to his aunty and his father.

إِنْ شَاءَ اللهُ - This was said by Sayyidunā Yūsuf ﷺ as a form of blessing. The Qur'ān states,

$$\text{وَلَا تَقُوْلَنَّ لِشَيْءٍ إِنِّى فَاعِلٌ ذٰلِكَ غَدًا إِلَّا أَنْ يَّشَاءَ اللهُ}$$

"And never say of anything, "Indeed, I will do that tomorrow, except (when adding), "If Allāh wills." (18:23–24)

آمِنِيْنَ - This was used to indicate that Egypt will be very comfortable and that Kan'ān would not even be remembered. When one migrates to another city, there are many challenges such as getting a new job, a new environment, new neighbours etc. Sayyidunā Yūsuf ﷺ is saying here you will all be 'royal'.

$$\text{وَرَفَعَ أَبَوَيْهِ عَلَى الْعَرْشِ وَخَرُّوا لَهُ سُجَّدًا ۚ وَقَالَ يَا أَبَتِ هٰذَا تَأْوِيْلُ رُؤْيَايَ مِنْ قَبْلُ قَدْ}$$
$$\text{جَعَلَهَا رَبِّى حَقًّا ۖ وَقَدْ أَحْسَنَ بِى إِذْ أَخْرَجَنِى مِنَ السِّجْنِ وَجَاءَ بِكُمْ مِّنَ الْبَدْوِ مِنْ بَعْدِ أَنْ}$$
$$\text{نَّزَغَ الشَّيْطَانُ بَيْنِى وَبَيْنَ إِخْوَتِى ۚ إِنَّ رَبِّى لَطِيْفٌ لِّمَا يَشَاءُ ۚ إِنَّهُ هُوَ الْعَلِيْمُ الْحَكِيْمُ}$$

[100] And he raised his parents up on the throne, and they all fell before him in prostration. He said, "My father, here is the interpretation of my early dream. My Lord has made it come true. He favoured me when he released me from the prison, and brought you (here) from bedouin life after Shaytān had caused a rift between me and my brothers. Surely, my Lord does what He

wills in a subtle way. Surely, He is the All-Knowing, the All-Wise."

Sayyidunā Yūsuf ﷺ raising his parents upon the throne is a lesson for us all that we should respect our parents and keep them happy. Despite Sayyidunā Yūsuf ﷺ being a king, he raised his father and respected him. When one of us is given a high status, we should not disregard our parents rather we should keep utmost respect for them.

وَخَرُّوۡالَهٗ سُجَّدًا - There are two types of Sajdah (prostration):

عِبَادَةٌ - Prostration for worship - This is solely for Allāh ﷻ and nobody else. It was not allowed in any previous nation nor is it allowed in this nation.

تَعۡظِيۡمٌ - Prostration for respect - This was allowed in previous nations however it is Harām (forbidden) in our Sharīah.

The above Sajdah (prostration) was of تَعۡظِيۡمٌ. Therefore, it was allowed in that era.

هٰذَاتَأۡوِيۡلُ رُءۡيَايَ مِنۡ قَبۡلُ - This refers to the dream which Sayyidunā Yūsuf ﷺ saw when he was a boy,

يَا أَبَتِ إِنِّي رَأَيْتُ أَحَدَ عَشَرَ كَوْكَبًا وَّالشَّمْسَ وَالْقَمَرَ رَأَيْتُهُمْ لِيْ سَاجِدِيْنَ

"O My father, I saw (in a dream) eleven stars, the sun and the moon; I saw them all prostrating before me." (12:4)

The eleven stars refers to the eleven brothers and the sun and the moon refers to the mother and father.

Sayyidunā Yūsuf ﷺ Praises Allāh ﷻ

رَبِّ قَدْ آتَيْتَنِيْ مِنَ الْمُلْكِ وَعَلَّمْتَنِيْ مِنْ تَأْوِيْلِ الْأَحَادِيْثِ ۚ فَاطِرَ السَّمَاوَاتِ وَالْأَرْضِ أَنتَ وَلِيِّيْ فِي الدُّنْيَا وَالْآخِرَةِ ۖ تَوَفَّنِيْ مُسْلِمًا وَّأَلْحِقْنِيْ بِالصَّالِحِيْنَ

[101] My Lord, You have given me (something) of sovereignty and taught me of the interpretation of dreams. Creator of the heavens and earth, You are my Protector in this world and in the Hereafter. Cause me to die a Muslim and join me with the right-eous."

Sayyidunā Yūsuf ﷺ thanks Allāh ﷻ for His immense favours and blessings, praises Him and invokes a good death– the death of a believer. We should always beg Allāh ﷻ to cause us to die as Muslims. Āmīn

ذَٰلِكَ مِنْ أَنْبَاءِ الْغَيْبِ نُوْحِيْهِ إِلَيْكَ ۖ وَمَا كُنْتَ لَدَيْهِمْ إِذْ أَجْمَعُوْا أَمْرَهُمْ وَهُمْ يَمْكُرُوْنَ

[102] That is from the news of the unseen which We reveal (O Muhammad) to you. And you were not with them when they put together their plan while they conspired.

وَمَا أَكْثَرُ النَّاسِ وَلَوْ حَرَصْتَ بِمُؤْمِنِينَ

[103] And most of the people, although you strive (for it), are not believers.

وَمَا تَسْأَلُهُمْ عَلَيْهِ مِنْ أَجْرٍ ۚ إِنْ هُوَ إِلَّا ذِكْرٌ لِّلْعَالَمِينَ

[104]And you do not ask of them for it any payment. It is not except a reminder to the worlds.

Signs of Allāh ﷻ

وَكَأَيِّن مِّنْ آيَةٍ فِي السَّمَاوَاتِ وَالْأَرْضِ يَمُرُّونَ عَلَيْهَا وَهُمْ عَنْهَا مُعْرِضُونَ

[105] And how many a sign within the heavens and earth do they pass over while they, therefrom are turning away.

وَمَا يُؤْمِنُ أَكْثَرُهُمْ بِاللهِ إِلَّا وَهُمْ مُشْرِكُونَ

[106] And most of them believe not in Allāh except while they associate others with Him.

أَفَأَمِنُوٓا أَن تَأْتِيَهُمْ غَاشِيَةٌ مِّنْ عَذَابِ اللّٰهِ أَوْ تَأْتِيَهُمُ السَّاعَةُ بَغْتَةً وَّهُمْ لَا يَشْعُرُونَ

[107] Then do they feel secure that there will not come to them an overwhelming (aspect) of the punishment of Allāh or that the Hour will not come upon them suddenly while they do not perceive?

In previous nations, when people would deny the message and truth of Islām, Allāh ﷻ would send a punishment destroying all. These places should not be visited except as an Ibrat (lesson). Places where Allāh's ﷻ curse and punishment has penetrated should be only visited as a reminder and admonition.

The Prophet ﷺ said to the Companions ﷺ when they were passing by the dwellings of the nation of Thamūd, "Do not enter the homes of those who have oppressed themselves except in a crying state, fearing that the punishment does not afflict you."

قُلْ هٰذِهِ سَبِيلِيٓ أَدْعُوٓا إِلَى اللّٰهِ عَلَىٰ بَصِيرَةٍ أَنَا وَمَنِ اتَّبَعَنِيْ وَسُبْحَانَ اللّٰهِ وَمَا أَنَا مِنَ الْمُشْرِكِيْنَ

[108] Say, "This is my way; I invite to Allāh with insight, I and those who follow me. And exalted is Allāh; and I am not of those who associate others with Him."

وَمَآ أَرْسَلْنَا مِن قَبْلِكَ إِلَّا رِجَالًا نُّوحِي إِلَيْهِم مِّنْ أَهْلِ الْقُرَىٰ ۗ أَفَلَمْ يَسِيرُوا فِي الْأَرْضِ فَيَنظُرُوا كَيْفَ كَانَ عَاقِبَةُ الَّذِينَ مِن قَبْلِهِمْ ۗ وَلَدَارُ الْآخِرَةِ خَيْرٌ لِّلَّذِينَ اتَّقَوْا ۗ أَفَلَا تَعْقِلُونَ

[109] And We sent not before you (as Messengers) except men to whom We revealed from among the people of cities. So have they not travelled through the earth and observed how was the end of those before them? And the home of the Hereafter is best for those who fear Allāh; then will you not reason?

Throughout history, Allāh ﷻ has sent Messengers with the same message, to guide the people. These Prophets and Messengers have always been male.

حَتَّىٰ إِذَا اسْتَيْأَسَ الرُّسُلُ وَظَنُّوا أَنَّهُمْ قَدْ كُذِبُوا جَاءَهُمْ نَصْرُنَا فَنُجِّيَ مَن نَّشَاءُ ۖ وَلَا يُرَدُّ بَأْسُنَا عَنِ الْقَوْمِ الْمُجْرِمِينَ

[110] (They continued) until, when the Messengers despaired and were certain that they had been denied, there came to them Our victory, and whoever We wanted was saved. And Our punishment cannot be repelled from the people who are criminals.

لَقَدْ كَانَ فِي قَصَصِهِمْ عِبْرَةٌ لِّأُولِي الْأَلْبَابِ ۗ مَا كَانَ حَدِيثًا يُفْتَرَىٰ وَلَٰكِن تَصْدِيقَ الَّذِي بَيْنَ يَدَيْهِ وَتَفْصِيلَ كُلِّ شَيْءٍ وَهُدًى وَرَحْمَةً لِّقَوْمٍ يُؤْمِنُونَ

[111] There was certainly in their stories a lesson for those of understanding. Never was the Qur'ān a narration invented, but a confirmation of what was before it and a detailed explanation of all things and guidance and mercy for the people who believe.

The Holy Qur'ān has always reinforced what was stated in the other Holy books, before they were tampered with. The story of Sayyidunā Yūsuf ﷷ is mentioned in other divine books as well.

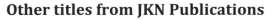

Other titles from JKN Publications

Your Questions Answered

An outstanding book written by Shaykh Mufti Saiful Islām. A very comprehensive yet simple Fatāwa book and a source of guidance that reaches out to a wider audience i.e. the English speaking Muslims. The reader will benefit from the various answers to questions based on the Laws of Islām relating to the beliefs of Islām, knowledge, Sunnah, pillars of Islām, marriage, divorce and contemporary issues.

UK RRP: £7.50

Hadeeth for Beginners

A concise Hadeeth book with various Ahādeeth that relate to basic Ibādāh and moral etiquettes in Islām accessible to a wider readership. Each Hadeeth has been presented with the Arabic text, its translation and commentary to enlighten the reader, its meaning and application in day-to-day life.

UK RRP: £3.00

Du'ā for Beginners

This book contains basic Du'ās which every Muslim should recite on a daily basis. Highly recommended to young children and adults studying at Islamic schools and Madrasahs so that one may cherish the beautiful treasure of supplications of our beloved Prophet ﷺ in one's daily life, which will ultimately bring peace and happiness in both worlds, Inshā-Allāh.

UK RRP: £2.00

How well do you know Islām?

An exciting educational book which contains 300 multiple questions and answers to help you increase your knowledge on Islām! Ideal for the whole family, especially children and adult students to learn new knowledge in an enjoyable way and cherish the treasures of knowledge that you will acquire from this book. A very beneficial tool for educational syllabus.

UK RRP: £3.00

Treasures of the Holy Qur'ān

This book entitled "Treasures of the Holy Qur'ān" has been compiled to create a stronger bond between the Holy Qur'ān and the readers. It mentions the different virtues of Sūrahs and verses from the Holy Qur'ān with the hope that the readers will increase their zeal and enthusiasm to recite and inculcate the teachings of the Holy Qur'ān into their daily lives.

UK RRP: £3.00

Marriage - A Complete Solution

Islām regards marriage as a great act of worship. This book has been designed to provide the fundamental teachings and guidelines of all what relates to the marital life in a simplified English language. It encapsulates in a nutshell all the marriage laws mentioned in many of the main reference books in order to facilitate their understanding and implementation.

UK RRP: £5.00

Pearls of Luqmān

This book is a comprehensive commentary of Sūrah Luqmān, written beautifully by Shaykh Mufti Saiful Islām. It offers the reader with an enquiring mind, abundance of advice, guidance, counselling and wisdom.

The reader will be enlightened by many wonderful topics and anecdotes mentioned in this book, which will create a greater understanding of the Holy Qur'ān and its wisdom. The book highlights some of the wise sayings and words of advice Luqmān ﷺ gave to his son.

UK RRP: £3.00

Arabic Grammar for Beginners

This book is a study of Arabic Grammar based on the subject of Nahw (Syntax) in a simplified English format. If a student studies this book thoroughly, he/she will develop a very good foundation in this field, Inshā-Allāh. Many books have been written on this subject in various languages such as Arabic, Persian and Urdu. However, in this day and age there is a growing demand for this subject to be available in English .

UK RRP: £3.00

A Gift to My Youngsters

This treasure filled book, is a collection of Islamic stories, morals and anecdotes from the life of our beloved Prophet ﷺ, his Companions ﷺ and the pious predecessors. The stories and anecdotes are based on moral and ethical values, which the reader will enjoy sharing with their peers, friends, families and loved ones.

"A Gift to My Youngsters" – is a wonderful gift presented to the readers personally, by the author himself, especially with the youngsters in mind. He has carefully selected stories and anecdotes containing beautiful morals, lessons and valuable knowledge and wisdom.

UK RRP: £5.00

Travel Companion

The beauty of this book is that it enables a person on any journey, small or distant or simply at home, to utilise their spare time to read and benefit from an exciting and vast collection of important and interesting Islamic topics and lessons. Written in simple and easy to read text, this book will immensely benefit both the newly interested person in Islām and the inquiring mind of a student expanding upon their existing knowledge. Inspiring reminders from the Holy Qur'ān and the blessed words of our beloved Prophet ﷺ beautifies each topic and will illuminate the heart of the reader.
UK RRP: £5.00

Pearls of Wisdom

Junaid Baghdādi ؓ once said, "Allāh ﷻ strengthens through these Islamic stories the hearts of His friends, as proven from the Qur'anic verse,
"And all that We narrate unto you of the stories of the Messengers, so as to strengthen through it your heart." (11:120)
Mālik Ibn Dinār ؓ stated that such stories are gifts from Paradise. He also emphasised to narrate these stories as much as possible as they are gems and it is possible that an individual might find a truly rare and invaluable gem among them.
UK RRP: £6.00

Inspirations

This book contains a compilation of selected speeches delivered by Shaykh Mufti Saiful Islam on a variety of topics such as the Holy Qur'ān, Nikāh and eating Halāl. Having previously been compiled in separate booklets, it was decided that the transcripts be gathered together in one book for the benefit of the reader. In addition to this, we have included in this book, further speeches which have not yet been printed.

UK RRP: £6.00

Gift to my Sisters

A thought provoking compilation of very interesting articles including real life stories of pious predecessors, imaginative illustrations and much more. All designed to influence and motivate mothers, sisters, wives and daughters towards an ideal Islamic lifestyle. A lifestyle referred to by our Creator, Allāh ﷻ in the Holy Qur'ān as the means to salvation and ultimate success.

UK RRP: £6.00

Gift to my Brothers

A thought provoking compilation of very interesting articles including real life stories of pious predecessors, imaginative illustrations, medical advices on intoxicants and rehabilitation and much more. All designed to influence and motivate fathers, brothers, husbands and sons towards an ideal Islamic lifestyle. A lifestyle referred to by our Creator, Allāh ﷻ in the Holy Qur'ān as the means to salvation and ultimate success.

UK RRP: £5.00

Heroes of Islām
"In the narratives there is certainly a lesson for people of intelligence (understanding)." (12:111)
A fine blend of Islamic personalities who have been recognised for leaving a lasting mark in the hearts and minds of people.
A distinguishing feature of this book is that the author has selected not only some of the most world and historically famous renowned scholars but also these lesser known and a few who have simply left behind a valuable piece of advice to their nearest and dearest. **UK RRP: £5.00**

Ask a Mufti (3 volumes)

Muslims in every generation have confronted different kinds of challenges. In-spite of that, Islām produced such luminary Ulamā who confronted and re-sponded to the challenges of their time to guide the Ummah to the straight path.
"Ask A Mufti" is a comprehensive three volume fatwa book, based on the Hanafi School, covering a wide range of topics related to every aspect of human life such as belief, ritual worship, life after death and contemporary legal topics related to purity, commercial transaction, marriage, divorce, food, cosmetic, laws pertaining to women, Islamic medical ethics and much more.
UK RRP: £30.00

Should I Follow a Madhab?
Taqleed or following one of the four legal schools is not a new phenomenon. Historically, scholars of great calibre and luminaries, each one being a specialist in his own right, were known to have adhered to one of the four legal schools. It is only in the previous century that a minority group emerged advocating a se-vere ban on following one of the four major schools.
This book endeavours to address the topic of Taqleed and elucidates its im-portance and necessity in this day and age. It will also, by the Divine Will of Allāh ﷻ dispel some of the confusion surrounding this topic. **UK RRP: £5.00**

Advice for the Students of Knowledge

Allāh ﷻ describes divine knowledge in the Holy Qur'ān as a 'Light'. Amongst the qualities of light are purity and guidance. The Holy Prophet ﷺ has clearly ex-plained this concept in many blessed Ahādeeth and has also taught us many supplications in which we ask for beneficial knowledge.
This book is a golden tool for every sincere student of knowledge wishing to mould his/her character and engrain those correct qualities in order to be wor-thy of receiving the great gift of Ilm from Allāh ﷻ. **UK RRP: £3.00**

Stories for Children
"Stories for Children" - is a wonderful gift presented to the readers personally by the author himself, especially with the young children in mind. The stories are based on moral and ethical values, which the reader will enjoy sharing with their peers, friends, families and loved ones. The aim is to present to the children stories and incidents which contain moral lessons, in order to reform and correct their lives, according to the Holy Qur'ān and Sunnah.
UK RRP: £5.00

Pearls from My Shaykh

This book contains a collection of pearls and inspirational accounts of the Holy Prophet ﷺ, his noble Companions, pious predecessors and some personal accounts and sayings of our well-known contemporary scholar and spiritual guide, Shaykh Mufti Saiful Islām Sāhib. Each anecdote and narrative of the pious predecessors have been written in the way that was narrated by Mufti Saiful Islām Sāhib in his discourses, drawing the specific lessons he intended from telling the story. The accounts from the life of the Shaykh has been compiled by a particular student based on their own experience and personal observation. **UK RRP: £5.00**

Paradise & Hell

This book is a collection of detailed explanation of Paradise and Hell including the state and conditions of its inhabitants. All the details have been taken from various reliable sources. The purpose of its compilation is for the reader to contemplate and appreciate the innumerable favours, rewards, comfort and unlimited luxuries of Paradise and at the same time take heed from the punishment of Hell. Shaykh Mufti Saiful Islām Sāhib has presented this book in a unique format by including the Tafseer and virtues of Sūrah Ar-Rahmān. **UK RRP: £5.00**

Prayers for Forgiveness

Prayers for Forgiveness' is a short compilation of Du'ās in Arabic with English translation and transliteration. This book can be studied after 'Du'ā for Beginners' or as a separate book. It includes twenty more Du'ās which have not been mentioned in the previous Du'ā book. It also includes a section of Du'ās from the Holy Qur'ān and a section from the Ahādeeth. The book concludes with a section mentioning the Ninety-Nine Names of Allāh ﷻ with its translation and transliteration. **UK RRP: £3.00**

Scattered Pearls

This book is a collection of scattered pearls taken from books, magazines, emails and WhatsApp messages. These pearls will hopefully increase our knowledge, wisdom and make us realise the purpose of life. In this book, Mufti Sāhib has included messages sent to him from scholars, friends and colleagues which will be beneficial and interesting for our readers Inshā-Allāh. **UK RRP: £4.00**

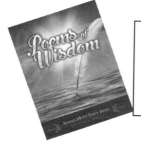

Poems of Wisdom

This book is a collection of poems from those who contributed to the Al-Mumin Magazine in the poems section. The Hadeeth mentions "Indeed some form of poems are full of wisdom." The themes of each poem vary between wittiness, thought provocation, moral lessons, emotional to name but a few. The readers will benefit from this immensely and make them ponder over the outlook of life in general.

UK RRP: £4.00

Horrors of Judgement Day
This book is a detailed and informative commentary of the first three Sūrahs of the last Juz namely; Sūrah Naba, Sūrah Nāzi'āt and Sūrah Abasa. These Sūrahs vividly depict the horrific events and scenes of the Great Day in order to warn mankind the end of this world. These Sūrahs are an essential reminder for us all to instil the fear and concern of the Day of Judgement and to detach ourselves from the worldly pleasures. Reading this book allows us to attain the true realization of this world and provides essential advices of how to gain eternal salvation in the Hereafter.

RRP: £5:00

Spiritual Heart
It is necessary that Muslims always strive to better themselves at all times and to free themselves from the destructive maladies. This book focusses on three main spiritual maladies; pride, anger and evil gazes. It explains its root causes and offers some spiritual cures. Many examples from the lives of the pious predecessors are used for inspiration and encouragement for controlling the above three maladies. It is hoped that the purification process of the heart becomes easy once the underlying roots of the above maladies are clearly understood.

UK RRP: £5:00

Hajj & Umrah for Beginners
This book is a step by step guide on Hajj and Umrah for absolute beginners. Many other additional important rulings (Masāil) have been included that will Insha-Allāh prove very useful for our readers. The book also includes some etiquettes of visiting (Ziyārat) of the Holy Prophet's ﷺ blessed Masjid and his Holy Grave.

UK RRP £3:00

Advice for the Spiritual Travellers
This book contains essential guidelines for a spiritual Murīd to gain some familiarity of the science of Tasawwuf. It explains the meaning and aims of Tasawwuf, some understanding around the concept of the soul, and general guidelines for a spiritual Murīd. This is highly recommended book and it is hoped that it gains wider readership among those Murīds who are basically new to the science of Tasawwuf.

UK RRP £3:00

Don't Worry Be Happy
This book is a compilation of sayings and earnest pieces of advice that have been gathered directly from my respected teacher Shaykh Mufti Saiful Islām Sāhib. The book consists of many valuable enlightenments including how to deal with challenges of life, promoting unity, practicing good manners, being optimistic and many other valuable advices. Our respected Shaykh has gathered this Naseehah from meditating, contemplating, analysing and searching for the gems within Qur'anic verses, Ahādeeth and teachings of our Pious Predecessors. **UK RRP £1:00**

Kanzul Bāri

Kanzul Bāri provides a detailed commentary of the Ahādeeth contained in Saheeh al-Bukhāri. The commentary includes Imām Bukhāri's ﷺ biography, the status of his book, spiritual advice, inspirational accounts along with academic discussions related to Fiqh, its application and differences of opinion. Moreover, it answers objections arising in one's mind about certain Ahādeeth. Inquisitive students of Hadeeth will find this commentary a very useful reference book in the final year of their Ālim course for gaining a deeper understanding of the science of Hadeeth. **UK RRP: £15.00**

How to Become a Friend of Allāh ﷺ

The friends of Allāh ﷺ have been described in detail in the Holy Qur'ān and Āhadeeth. This book endeavours its readers to help create a bond with Allāh ﷺ in attaining His friendship as He is the sole Creator of all material and immaterial things. It is only through Allāh's ﷺ friendship, an individual will achieve happiness in this life and the Hereafter, hence eliminate worries, sadness, depression, anxiety and misery of this world. **UK RRP:**

Gems & Jewels

This book contains a selection of articles which have been gathered for the benefit of the readers covering a variety of topics on various aspects of daily life. It offers precious advice and anecdotes that contain moral lessons. The advice captivates its readers and will extend the narrowness of their thoughts to deep reflection, wisdom and appreciation of the purpose of our existence. **UK RRP: £4.00**

End of Time

This book is a comprehensive explanation of the three Sūrahs of Juzz Amma; Sūrah Takweer, Sūrah Infitār and Sūrah Mutaffifeen. This book is a continuation from the previous book of the same author, 'Horrors of Judgement Day'. The three Sūrahs vividly sketch out the scene of the Day of Judgement and describe the state of both the inmates of Jannah and Jahannam. Mufti Saiful Islām Sāhib provides an easy but comprehensive commentary of the three Sūrahs facilitating its understanding for the readers whilst capturing the horrific scene of the ending of the world and the conditions of mankind on that horrific Day.

Golden Legacy of Spain

Andalus (modern day Spain), the long lost history, was once a country that produced many great calibre of Muslim scholars comprising of Mufassirūn, Muhaddithūn, Fuqahā, judges, scientists, philosophers, surgeons, to name but a few. The Muslims conquered Andalus in 711 AD and ruled over it for eight-hundred years. This was known as the era of Muslim glory. Many non-Muslim Europeans during that time travelled to Spain to study under Muslim scholars. The remanences of the Muslim rule in Spain are manifested through their universities, magnificent palaces and Masājid carved with Arabic writings, standing even until today. In this book, Shaykh Mufti Saiful Islām shares some of his valuable experiences he witnessed during his journey to Spain. **UK RRP: £3.00**

Ideal Youth

This book contains articles gathered from various social media avenues; magazines, emails, WhatsApp and telegram messages that provide useful tips of advice for those who have the zeal to learn and consider changing their negative habits and behavior and become better Muslims to set a positive trend for the next generation. **UK RRP:£4:00**

Ideal Teacher

This book contains abundance of precious advices for the Ulamā who are in the teaching profession. It serves to present Islamic ethical principles of teaching and to remind every teacher of their moral duties towards their students. This book will Inshā-Allāh prove to be beneficial for newly graduates and scholars wanting to utilize their knowledge through teaching. **UK RRP:£4:00**

Ideal Student

This book is a guide for all students of knowledge in achieving the excellent qualities of becoming an ideal student. It contains precious advices, anecdotes of our pious predecessors and tips in developing good morals as a student. Good morals is vital for seeking knowledge. A must for all students if they want to develop their Islamic Knowledge. **UK RRP:£4:00**

Ideal Parents

This book contains a wealth of knowledge in achieving the qualities of becoming ideal parents. It contains precious advices, anecdotes of our pious predecessors and tips in developing good parenthood skills. Good morals is vital for seeking knowledge. A must for all parents . **UK RRP:£4:00**

Ideal Couple

This book is a compilation of inspiring stories and articles containing useful tips and life skills for every couple. Marriage life is a big responsibility and success in marriage is only possible if the couple know what it means to be an ideal couple. **UK RRP:£4:00**

Ideal Role Model

This book is a compilation of sayings and accounts of our pious predecessors. The purpose of this book is so we can learn from our pious predecessors the purpose of this life and how to attain closer to the Creator. Those people who inspires us attaining closeness to our Creator are our true role models. A must everyone to read. **UK RRP:£4:00**

Bangladesh– A Land of Natural Beauty

This book is a compilation of our respected Shaykh's journeys to Bangladesh including visits to famous Madāris and Masājid around the country. The Shaykh shares some of his thought provoking experiences and his personal visits with great scholars in Bangladesh. **UK RRP: £4.00**

Pearls from the Qur'an

This series begins with the small Sūrahs from 30th Juzz initially, unravelling its heavenly gems, precious advices and anecdotes worthy of personal reflection. It will most definitely benefit both those new to as well as advanced students of the science of Tafsīr. The purpose is to make it easily accessible for the general public in understanding the meaning of the Holy Qur'ān. **UK RRP: £10.00**

When the Heavens Split

This book contains the commentary of four Sūrahs from Juzz Amma namely; Sūrah Inshiqāq, Sūrah Burūj, Sūrah Tāriq and Sūrah A'lā. The first two Sūrahs contain a common theme of capturing the scenes and events of the Last Day and how this world will come to an end. However, all four Sūrahs mentioned, have a connection of the journey of humanity, reflection on nature, how nature changes and most importantly, giving severe warnings to mankind about the punishments and exhorting them to prepare for the Hereafter through good deeds and refraining from sins. **UK RRP: £4.00**

The Lady who Spoke the Qur'ān

The Holy Prophet ﷺ was sent as a role model who was the physical form of the Holy Qur'ān. Following the ways of the Holy Prophet ﷺ in every second of our lives is pivotal for success. This booklet tells us the way to gain this success. It also includes an inspirational incident of an amazing lady who only spoke from the Holy Qur'an throughout her life. We will leave it to our readers to marvel at her intelligence, knowledge and piety expressed in this breath-taking episode. **UK RRP:£3:00**

Dearest Act to Allāh

Today our Masājid have lofty structures, engraved brickworks, exquisite chandeliers and laid rugs, but they are spiritually deprived due to the reason that the Masājid are used for social purposes including backbiting and futile talk rather than the performance of Salāh, Qur'ān recitation and the spreading of true authentic Islamic knowledge. This book elaborates on the etiquettes of the Masjid and the importance of Salāh with Quranic and prophetic proofs along with some useful anecdotes to emphasize their importance. **UK RRP:£3:00**

Don't Delay Your Nikāh

Marriage plays an important role in our lives. It is a commemoration of the union of two strangers who will spend the rest of their remaining lives with one another. Marriage ought to transpire comfort and tranquillity whereby the couple share one another's sorrow and happiness. It is strongly recommended that our brothers and sisters read and benefit from this book and try to implement it into our daily lives in order to once more revive the Sunnah of the Holy Prophet ﷺ on such occasions and repel the prevalent sins and baseless customs.
UK RRP:£3:00

Miracle of the Holy Qur'ān

The scholars of Islām are trying to wake us all up, however, we are busy dreaming of the present world and have forgotten our real destination. Shaykh Mufti Saiful Islām Sāhib has been conducted Tafsīr of the Holy Qur'ān every week for almost two decades with the purpose of reviving its teachings and importance. This book is a transcription of two titles; Miracle of the Holy Qur'ān and The Revelation of the Holy Qur'ān, both delivered during the weekly Tafsīr sessions. **UK RRP:£3:00**

You are what you Eat

Eating Halāl and earning a lawful income plays a vital role in the acceptance of all our Ibādāt (worship) and good deeds. Mufti Saiful Islām Sāhib has presented a discourse on this matter in one of his talks. I found the discourse to be very beneficial, informative and enlightening on the subject of Halāl and Harām that clarifies its importance and status in Islām. I strongly recommend my Muslim brothers and sisters to read this treatise and to study it thoroughly.
UK RRP:£3:00

Sleepers of the Cave

The Tafsīr of Sūrah Kahf is of crucial importance in this unique and challenging time we are currently living in. This book is evidently beneficial for all Muslims, more crucial for the general public. This is because Mufti Sāhib gives us extensive advice on how to act accordingly when treading the path of seeking knowledge. Readers will find amazing pieces of advice in terms of etiquettes regarding seeking knowledge and motivation, Inshā-Allāh. **UK RRP:£5:00**

Contentment of the Heart

The purification of the soul and its rectification are matters of vital importance which were brought by our Holy Prophet e to this Ummah. The literal meaning of Tazkiyah is 'to cleanse'. The genuine Sūfis assert that the foundation and core of all virtuous character is sincerity and the basis for all evil characteristics and traits is love for this world. This book endeavors to address certain spiritual maladies and how to overcome them using Islamic principles. **UK RRP:£5:00**

Contemporary Fiqh

This book is a selection of detailed *Fiqhi* (juridical) articles on contemporary legal issues. These detailed articles provide an in depth and elaborative response to some of the queries posted to us in our Fatawa department over the last decade. The topics discussed range between purity, domestic issues, Halāl and Harām, Islamic medical ethics, marital issues, rituals and so forth. Many of the juristic cases are unprecedented as a result of the ongoing societal changes and newly arising issues. **UK RRP:£6:00**

Ideal Society

In this book, 'Ideal Society' which is a commentary of Sūrah Hujurāt, Shaykh Mufti Saiful Islām Sāhib explains the lofty status of our beloved Prophet ﷺ, the duties of the believers and general mankind and how to live a harmonious social life, which is free from evil, jealousy and vices. Inshā-Allāh, this book will enable and encourage the readers to adopt a social life which will ultimately bring happiness and joy to each and every individual.

UK RRP:£5:00